Dslr Photography

A Comprehensive Beginner's Guide to Learning About Digital Slr Photography

(Simple and Easy Principles and Techniques to Taking Great Photographs With Your Dslr)

Jason Clark

Published By **John Kembrey**

Jason Clark

All Rights Reserved

Dslr Photography: A Comprehensive Beginner's Guide to Learning About Digital Slr Photography (Simple and Easy Principles and Techniques to Taking Great Photographs With Your Dslr)

ISBN 978-1-998901-06-7

No part of this guidebook shall be reproduced in any form without permission in writing from the publisher except in the case of brief quotations embodied in critical articles or reviews.

Legal & Disclaimer

The information contained in this ebook is not designed to replace or take the place of any form of medicine or professional medical advice. The information in this ebook has been provided for educational & entertainment purposes only.

The information contained in this book has been compiled from sources deemed reliable, and it is accurate to the best of the Author's knowledge; however, the Author cannot guarantee its accuracy and validity and cannot be held liable for any errors or omissions. Changes are periodically made to this book. You must consult your doctor or get professional medical advice before using any of the suggested remedies, techniques, or information in this book.

Upon using the information contained in this book, you agree to hold harmless the Author from and against any damages, costs, and expenses, including any legal fees potentially resulting from the application of any of the information provided by this guide. This disclaimer applies to any damages or injury caused by the use and application, whether directly or indirectly, of any advice or information presented, whether for breach of contract, tort, negligence, personal injury, criminal intent, or under any other cause of action.

You agree to accept all risks of using the information presented inside this book. You need to consult a professional medical practitioner in order to ensure you are both able and healthy enough to participate in this program.

Table Of Contents

Chapter 1: Manual Mode: Dial M

Modes

Most DSLR cameras come with a dial that can be used to change settings. To change modes on the camera, you can turn the dial. You also have many options to choose from for when you are ready to take pictures. The Manual Mode will be the focus of this chapter. But we'll also cover all other modes that your camera offers. We'll be covering the main modes found on most cameras along with those that will most benefit beginners. We recommend you work your way up to manual mode, or start there if that is what you are most comfortable with. This mode is the best way to get into photography. You can still use the other modes, but these are only a sample of the whole of photography. It can be frustrating for both your creativity as well and your growth as a professional photographer to let the camera decide what you want. The other modes aren't necessarily useless but don't offer the same freedom and experience as the manual mode.

These are only a few examples of specialty modes and video modes available on some cameras. Each camera is unique and serves a specific purpose. The camera's cost also has an impact on the features it offers. The following list can be used as a guide to the most popular modes that you will find on any DSLR.

Auto Mode

When you are starting to learn the basics of your DSLR, auto mode is a great way to begin. But, you won't be able to get the most from your DSLR if this is where you start. The camera controls all settings including shutter speed, ISO and exposure. This mode allows you to quickly and easily use your camera.

Auto mode can produce some amazing shots but only so much. The photographer does not have any control over how the camera decides. As the camera makes all the decisions, you cannot control how your image is composed.

This mode will produce lovely, simple shots but you have limited creative options. If you are looking to paint with light in a night shoot, this mode is the best. Auto mode wouldn't let you open the shutter long enough to do this. It would aim for the best exposure possible of whatever you are photographing. Auto mode will provide clear, well-lit shots. Let's also consider action shots taken at sporting events. The shutter speed that freezes the motion may not be fast enough for an auto mode with the best exposure. Most of the time, blurry players at the court or on the field won't relay the story the photographer wishes to tell. While auto mode can be a great place, once you're comfortable with your camera it's important that your creativity is explored in all modes. Imagine a whole new world if your imagination is strong enough to continue turning the dial.

Macro Mode

Macro mode can be used to adjust the depth-of-field and focus settings so you can capture closeups. Macro shots usually have the subject taking up a large portion of the frame. To blur the background or cover it with bokeh, macro shots are often taken. These are light circles that appear in shallow depths of field images. It is a lovely effect and can add a sense whimsy, or even mystery to close up shots.

Auto mode is useful to capture plants, insects, or other small objects, but not for any other photography. It's only intended for one purpose and should not be used elsewhere. It's a great mode to explore different compositions in your photographs and learn the effects of a shallow field of focus. To continue your photographic development, you must keep using macro modes.

Landscape Mode

Landscape mode will enable you to get the most out a scene that you are trying. You can use a tripod to help you get the best out of this mode. Depending on the environment, the camera's meters will decide which combination of shutter speed (f stop) and ISO is most effective to capture the image. The mode does not allow for much experimentation beyond composition. Although it is useful to keep track of the settings you use for shots that don't turn out as you wish, This will help you when you explore images you have total control of.

Consider the qualities of each shot you enjoyed and how ISO, fstop, and shutter speed contributed to these images.

Night Mode

Night mode can be used to shoot in low-light conditions like night. You will notice a slow shutter speed in this mode. Therefore, it is important to use tripod to avoid camera shake.

The shutter speed determines the way light is captured in the image. You might see some playful movement depending on your subject. If the shutter is open for longer time and the shutter speed is slow, any light moving through the frame will be captured in trails.

This mode can also use flash automatically if the camera determines it necessary. This will add to the subtle lighting effects found in the shot.

This effect can be used by photographers to create art with the light. It's a great effect to experiment with. But, the camera still has most of control so you won't get far in night mode. Take note of the images you like, and the settings that led to them. It will be an invaluable resource when you are attempting to capture images that you can control.

Sport Mode

Sport mode is useful for quickly and accurately taking action and moving objects. The camera freezes the action using a fast shutter speed. It is extremely useful for photographing sports or other events.

Sport mode is the same as all the other presets. However, it offers limited control. This makes it difficult to create compositions and allows you to freeze the action on the courts or fields. It is useful when you need quick shots and don't want to miss any moment due to blur. As you become more proficient with your DSLR, you will be better able to produce similar results and maintain greater control.

Portrait Mode

Portrait mode is best if you are shooting a still subject, which is the central point of your shot. This mode allows the camera to use a shallow depth effect to draw attention towards the subject, typically a person. This mode is not recommended for portrait photography, but it does have a limited range.

Priority: Aperture

Aperture priority mode lets you set the shutter speed and ISO, but the camera will control the f stop. This mode allows you to practice and experiment with the aperture. This determines your depth of field. This mode lets you select the aperture you would like to use and then the shutter speed and ISO are set by the camera. While you may not have full control of the camera, this mode allows you to practice each shot and learn about the various elements. It is a great way to practice with different settings and learn how they affect your image. You can practice using a priority mode like this to get familiar with the settings.

Shutter Priority

Shutter priority mode functions in the same way that aperture mode. In this mode you control the shutter speed. The camera handles f stop, ISO. Learn the effects shutter speed has on this mode by practicing. Try your hand at painting with light.

This is another great way to get familiar with your camera, and the art of photographing.

Program Mode

Program mode allows you modify and control the ISO and white balance as well as metering. The camera adjusts the shutter speed, aperture, and white balance based upon your settings.

No Flash

You can find a no-flash setting in the settings. This menu allows to turn off your flash, so that it does not activate under any circumstance. With this assurance, you won't be surprised when the flash turns on while you are shooting. A simple setting like this can help save photos from being lost.

Manual Mode

Manual mode, the focus of this chapter gives you the best control when shooting. In manual mode, you control the aperture and shutter speed to create the image of your dreams. The camera makes no decisions. Each decision is up to you. Although manual mode may seem overwhelming at the beginning, you will soon become more comfortable using your DSLR and the art.

Manual Mode: What's the point?

Why do you need manual mode? Isn't it easier to allow the camera to make all the decisions for us? This way, shooting would be very simple. You might be disappointed if the camera's presets are all you use to make your photos look good. You wouldn't be able take full control of your photography and learn the skills required to fully immerse yourself into the art of photojournalism if you let the camera make the decisions. Sometimes the camera may attempt to take you in a different direction than you intended. With a solid understanding of manual mode you can manipulate the camera to get any kind of image that you want. These are just some benefits to learning manual mode.

Creativity

Manual mode is the best option for creativity. You have complete control over the way you set up your camera. When the camera is in auto mode, or any other mode where it makes the decisions for the photographer's safety, its goal is to create the most exposure. This means that the camera meters the shot to attempt to illuminate the focal points (where you are pointing your camera) to their best advantage. The camera does not always succeed. There are many things that can go wrong with exposure when the camera is in control.

It could be that your subject has been backlit. Your shot may be exposed for the background rather than your subject. Sometimes your subject may be well lit but the background dark. The camera might overexpose your shot if it detects a dark background.

It will be challenging for the camera in unusual lighting situations. The result could surprise you. You're at the mercy the camera's limited knowledge and creativity. These errors would be eliminated if you could control the metering settings and how they would affect your situation.

A lot of great shots can only be achieved if you go beyond what the camera's sensor would consider a good exposure. With ordinary exposures, it is impossible to create silhouettes, bright lighting, and dark darks. The meter attempts to show the best lighting in each shot. Although the camera's meter is susceptible to getting confused, you will still be able capture stunning shots by yourself, even without auto mode. You have all the control in manual mode. It is up to the camera to decide what kind of exposure they want. The photographer may not be able to capture the story they are trying to tell with a typical exposure. Manual mode gives you the ability to express your thoughts through your photos, regardless of how the camera perceives them.

Exposure Regulation

Cameras that shoot in auto mode choose the settings based off the metering they read. These settings can change quickly. The right exposure can change depending on how difficult the lighting is or whether the subject is moving.

You will have inconsistent photos if your camera is set to auto in this type situation. Exposures will be affected by the changing light and subject. Imagine a bench sitting under a tree, with its branches shifting. As the light filters through leaves and branches, your camera will need a different exposure to where you are aiming. Because of the changing environment, each shot will look different so you can take several shots.

Manual mode allows you maintain consistent exposures no matter what the environment. Again, consider the bench that is under the tree. Manual mode lets you choose whether you want the bench to be shot in direct sunlight or in shade. This will enable you to accurately measure the lighting conditions and keep your settings in place as you shoot. This will give your peace of mind by knowing exactly what you will get for each shot.

As you improve your DSLR photography skills, consistency will come in handy. Inconsistency in your shots and confusion about what to expect can slow down your progression. It is possible to predict how your shot will turn out at any given point in time. This will allow you to master photography and learn how to control your settings so you get the best image. Also, consistent exposure is key when you are shooting a series.

Without consistent exposure, shots will not match. While this won't be an issue when you first start shooting, it is something to remember as your move into manual mode.

Summary of the Manual Mode Benefits

The photographer has the most control of their shots. This allows them to pick how each photo will look. Although there are no surprises once you're familiar with it, it can be difficult to keep track of. Manual mode can be daunting for beginners but is easy to master. It becomes easier and more natural to use, so you can take full control of your photo projects.

Others modes may look appealing because they take some of that pressure off when it is time to set up shots. But the effort you put into shooting in manual mode, once you are satisfied with what has been achieved, will pay off. You have total control of the creative and technical aspects of your photos. There is nothing more satisfying than this.

Chapter 2: The Exposure Triangle

What is the Triangle, exactly?

It is important to have a good understanding of exposure in order to fully appreciate manual photography. An understanding of the exposure triangle is necessary. The exposure triangular is comprised of shutter speed, aperture, ISO. Each element makes up one part of the triangle. They must all be aligned for the triangle's strength. Knowing how they interact is essential to success in photography. A balanced triangle is essential to ensure that your image's exposure is not too low. It can be damaged by either over- or underexposure.

Each triangle element works in conjunction with the others to create the ideal exposure for any shot. This is because there is a balance which creates this exposure. As with any equation or balancing act pieces can be changed without destroying exposure. You must remember that even if one component changes, another element must also be changed to maintain balance. The image must have the same elements if it is to come out right. Although it may seem difficult at first, this concept is simple once you understand it. However, it can be quite easy to apply to photography after some practice.

After we have presented the three sides and the triangle of exposure, we will dive into these issues in the next chapter. Before we go into detail, let us mention stop. Stop is fundamental to understanding all aspects of exposure we will discuss.

Stop

Stop is the amount you need to get a particular exposure. This number is subject to change and can vary from shot-to-shot as each photo is unique. It also depends on the lighting conditions. This amount is called the stop. Any light that changes will cause the photo to change. This is called adding or subtracting stop. Your photo will be altered regardless of whether you add or subtract. The image could be balanced, or even improved if it's done correctly. Neglecting to do so will result in overexposed photos or underexposed photos.

The exposure of your camera is affected by the addition or removal of stops. This will result in a double or halved amount light reaching the sensor. A stop can double the amount of light, resulting in a brighter shot. Add a stop to reduce the amount of light, your shot will become darker. If done correctly this can be used to your benefit.

You will need to be familiarized with this term in order for you to understand how each side of the exposure triangle interacts and decide the type of shot you end up with. The concept of stops will be essential when you start manipulating photos and exposures. By adding or subtracting those, you will end up with a picture. The goal is to be able and effective to use this to produce the desired photo.

The Sides of the Triangle

We will now look at the different sides. This chapter is an introduction to each side. We will cover them more in the subsequent chapters. It is important to get a good understanding of each side and how they contribute to the capture of photographs. Each task is essential to creating a good picture. Each has its unique benefits and can help you get the best possible shot at the end.

ISO

ISO refers the way your digital camera's sensors react to light. The term refers to film cameras. However, this process has changed. We will get into that more later.

The exposure triangle has two sides. Each number is proportional to the effect. The higher the number, the less light is required to create a good exposure. Doubling the number is equivalent to adding a stop. Halfing the number reduces that stop. The higher the number, brighter is the image. However, it's also possible to do the opposite.

You will likely not alter the ISO as much as you do the shutter speed and the f stop. However, you will still be trying out different ISO settings and making adjustments to achieve the desired photos. The ISO will dictate how the final product looks, but it won't be as useful when making minor adjustments to an image as fstop and shutter speed. But it is essential to be familiar with the ISO concept and its role as it will eventually affect the outcome of your photos.

Shutter Speed

Shutter speed affects the amount of time your shutter remains open. This is partly responsible for how much light reaches your digital sensor.

Shutter speed is the most obvious of all sides of the exposure triangle. The speed can be measured in seconds and fractions. The shutter must be open longer to let more light reach the sensor. A stop is a time multiplier that doubles the amount of light reaching the sensor. For example, if your shutter speed was 1/30s and you wanted to add a stop to it, your number would be doubled and the speed would change to 1/15s. It is the reverse. You would shoot at 1/60s if you had started at 1/30s.

While this may appear confusing at first, it is important to remember that shutter speed only works with fractions. Your shot will be more affected if your shutter is open for longer. You might be able to see objects or movements in the frame. It is because faster shutter speeds (described by smaller fractions), work best when there is sufficient light. In a later chapter, we'll discuss this more.

Remember, shutter speed not only affects the amount light that you expose but also the effect motion and action have on your final image.

F Stop

F stop, also known by the name aperture, is the size of an opening that allows light to enter the sensor. The aperture can be adjusted by you. This affects how much light gets to the sensor.

Doubling the aperture doubles light penetration and adds stop. The size of the aperture can be reduced by half and the light allowed through will decrease by one-half.

The problem with aperture is that it's not as simple to determine the opening's dimensions as you might expect. The smaller the number, it is. Both the numbers and their sums do not equal perfect doubling, halving. We'll explore the reasons for this in a separate chapter. We will get into the reasons why this is the case in a later chapter.

It is essential to remember though that fstop is primarily concerned with light (similarly to the other elements) along with the depth and field of each individual photo.

You need to keep your exposure balanced

A good exposure involves finding the settings for each of three sides of the triangle that are correct metering your shot. Another important aspect of a good exposure is how you want to present your shot artistically.

The bottom line, once you have chosen the best exposure for your subject, any element that needs to be changed must follow. If your shutter speed is increased by one stop, you must also decrease the ISO or aperture. Another example would be to decrease your aperture two stops. There would be two options to balance your exposure. Everything must be even. You can increase your ISO and shutter speed one at a time or two at a time. Both of these solutions would equalize the results. This rule will ensure that exposure is constant. The final shot will be very similar. The other way around is that deciding the exposure triangle's one element will affect the rest. The stage will be set for the other elements.

You might wonder why anyone would want to choose one side of the exposure triangular over another. Wouldn't if it were easier to stick with one element? The limit on the types of photos that can be produced by consistently choosing one element will be hard to achieve.

Each triangle effect affects one aspect of the shot. While we'll go into greater detail on each component later, we'll briefly explain the purpose of each here. The shutter speed has a direct effect on the motion of your photos. According to the speed of objects in motion, slower shutter speeds can freeze motion. Faster shutter speeds will freeze motion. F stop refers to the depth in which your photo will be covered. The smaller the aperture opening, it is, the deeper the depth of the field. This blurred background effect can be achieved by making the aperture wider. ISO refers to digital noise. This can also be referred to as grain. The grainier the image is, the greater the digital noise. Larger ISOs produce more grain.

There will be many shots where you need to focus on one part of the exposure triangle. Knowing how to prioritize your images will help you improve as a photographer. By practicing, you'll be able identify which element should be highlighted in your photos. This is a skill that takes practice, just like any other worthwhile skill. However, it will pay off in long term when you can amaze yourself and others with stunning photography.

Finding the Right Exposure

You will need to adjust the exposure of each shot depending on what type of photo it is. Experimenting will help you discover the right exposures for your photos. The best way to improve your photography skills is to practice. There is no one solution to every problem in photography. The exposure triangle balance does not provide a perfect answer. It may take some time to become familiar with the best techniques for getting the images you want as a beginner.

Metering can tell you the exposure for the shot in front of your camera. You can get an external handheld meter with most cameras. Your preference will depend on the type of meter you choose. Camera meters will still measure distance from subject. Camera meters will read where you point. A handheld spot meter allows you to take a closer look at what you are trying to measure and obtain a more accurate reading without needing to move the camera. General metering tells you the right settings to expose your shot well. Try to maintain an even exposure. Spot meters allow you to measure the lightest and darkest areas of your photo, then set your camera accordingly. This allows you to experiment with each side and adjust the exposure. The main focus is usually on aperture, shutter speed, and how your image is exposed.

In later chapters we will discuss how to determine which triangle element is best for what type of shot. The more you practice understanding how all three elements work together in the exposure triangle, the easier it will be to use your camera. Each element is essential to know, but it is crucial to get familiar with their interactions while serving the purpose of the shot. The exposure triangle forms the basis of DSLR photography. Without this understanding, it is difficult to predict and manipulate exposures accurately.

Why do I Need the Exposure Triangle

It may be easiest to simply focus on the basics of pointing and shooting. The camera will take over the rest and you can relax. Keep in mind that your purpose for reading this book is not to teach you how to take better photos.

By switching to manual mode, you can produce more variety and creativity. Understanding the exposure triangle is essential to fully benefit from this freedom. You will be able to see the exposure triangle and the individual elements as we go along in later chapters. This will give you a lot of options as a beginner photographer.

Don't be discouraged by the daunting mountain of information that can sometimes seem too difficult to navigate. Every great photographer started at the beginning. Every great photographer started with the exposure triangular. Every great photographer moved forward.

Chapter 3: Going With The Grain In Iso

What is ISO?

Before we discuss the uses and benefits of ISO, it is important for you to know its purpose and the actual meaning of this component of the Exposure Triangle. It stands for International Organization of Standardization. While this serves our purposes, it does not serve any other purpose than to give us an origin of the term that goes back in time to its roots in film photography. This is important to remember, because even though digital cameras exist today, ISO's principles still hold true, even though they refer to film.

ISO stands for ISO speed. In film cameras it refers both to the film's sensitivity to light and the type of picture that this sensitivity will allow you create. So, ISO speed is labeled on all rolls of film. This allows the photographer to identify how to set their camera's ISO with each roll of film. Photographers using film cameras should still correct their ISO everytime they change films to ensure their exposures are consistent. The ISO can be wrongly set and an image could end up being either too or too dark depending on when it was taken. The grain is irrelevant here (which we will discuss in this chapter) but the incorrect exposure.

The error can cause an otherwise stunning photo to become unusable. Great care should be taken to avoid this. Particularly for film cameras, this could lead to the destruction of whole rolls of film. The same error can happen with digital cameras. ISO is not one that you want to see at the top. It's not always visible on the camera screen so it can be easy for people to overlook it. It is not as destructive as it is in film cameras. However, it can lead to frustrating delays and wasted time if it is not handled properly.

Digital cameras come with an ISO. These numbers represent the same ISO levels that are found in film cameras. This is to give us all photographers a standard to work by. ISO can technically be used to refer to both film cameras or DSLRs but digital camera ISOs mimic the system of the film camera.

ISO is not the easiest element in your DSLR's menu system to understand. However, it is not the most difficult. For DSLRs with digital sensors, ISO does not directly refer to the sensitivity of your camera's sensor. ISO serves its original purpose. It allows you to decide how dark or bright your shot will appear. This is accomplished by replicating the effects of different ISOs in a film camera. ISO also makes a difference in each photograph you take, just like the two other sides of the exposure triangle.

Basic Effects in a Photo
Simply stated, ISO can either lighten or darken your shot. Stops work in a similar manner for ISO as for shutter speed. ISO numbers are sometimes referred to simply as speeds. To brighten your photo and double the light, add a stop or double the speed. The same applies to decreasing a stop. This reduces speed and darkens the photo by halving it.

ISO numbers can be adjusted from 100 to 6400. There are many options. Adjusting ISO is not something you want to do all the time. However, it can give more freedom to adjust your shutter speed and/or fstop. You can adjust ISO when you need more control over your shutter speed, your fstop, and/or both.

It is possible to find the right speed for your photograph depending on your personal preferences and image quality. Different ISO settings can have different effects on the quality of your shot. Take your gut instinct into consideration and see what shots you get.

Although this is true, I think many photographers would agree that you need to keep an image of high quality to achieve well-exposed images. A photo that has too much grain would be unprofessional, regardless of its composition or the quality of other elements in it, would not look good. Photographs that do not meet this quality standard will appear less professional and less eye-catching. Even the most thoughtful aesthetic decision could not save a photo that has been distorted or saturated by grain. This would mean that all hope was lost. These guidelines will help you improve your photography, and keep you on track through beginner to advanced levels.

Image Quality, ISO

The ISO speed can have a major impact on your image's quality. The greater the ISO number, you will have more digital noise. Digital noise can also be called grain. Although grain can sometimes be used to enhance an image's artistic look, it can cause damage. High ISO speeds can create grainy images, as well as blotchiness in the color of your shot.

There are two possible ways you can use ISO (high and low), each with its own advantages. Later, we'll talk about how to adjust ISO. But, for now, let's just focus on the impacts different ISO levels have upon image quality. We'll begin with a very high ISO.

Use high ISO only when it is absolutely necessary to have a fast shutter speed. These settings can be used to freeze motion when you're trying to capture it in an image. For action to be captured, a fast shutter speed is required. However, the shutter only lets in as much light as it needs. A higher ISO will be required in these situations to ensure adequate light is allowed to make a good exposure. ISOs higher than normal can also be necessary for low-light conditions. You might be shooting at night or in an auditorium with low lighting for a live event. Your camera must be mobile so that you can set the shutter speed quickly enough to prevent camera shake. The ISO setting must be adjusted to ensure exposure. ISO can prove to be an invaluable tool in such circumstances.

If you want to achieve the best image quality, it is possible to use a low ISO. A sharp, crisp image is possible by using a lower ISO. The base ISO is what your camera can use to set the lowest ISO. This will guarantee the best possible image quality for your camera. Although many cameras can reduce ISO to 100 on newer models, others are limited to 200. If you have enough light, you can take clear photos with no noise or grain. It is a good thing to start with the ISO base ISO. Then, work your way down. The choice of the right shutter speed can make all or part of a shoot.

Find the perfect balance to achieve the highest quality image

Finding the best exposure triangle for each shot is the key to great photography. Sometimes this means sacrifice of one element for another to improve the overall photo.

An easy way to tackle this dilemma is to determine your f stop. This will allow you to control your depth of field. Once you are satisfied, set your camera at the ISO base setting and adjust the shutter speed accordingly to your exposure. Finally, take a look at your shot. You should increase the ISO if your subject appears blurry. Once you have reached the ISO limit, adjust the aperture. The balance act is crucial. This is not an easy task. But you must make a decision. A photo's main element must be prioritized over other elements. It may be that the shutter speed is more important than the depth of the field, which you believed would improve the image. You might have needed a faster shutter speed to get the shot you wanted.

You will need to decide which elements will play a supporting role in your final photo and which one will shine. As blurry athletes are not what you want to photograph, action shots will have a priority shutter speed. Macro shots should be shot at f stop. The depth of the field is crucial in macro shots. ISO tends to change the most when strange lighting situations occur that require a specific setting. Your final decision as a photographer is yours. It is up you and your artistic (and perhaps experimental) imaginations how you want the sides to connect. However, keep in mind that the ISO value you set will influence how sharp the image. This knowledge will prove to be beneficial in your photographic endeavors.

How to Change Your ISO

Your ISO setting process can differ from one camera to the next. Some cameras require users open a menu to access the ISO settings. These mazes can quickly test the user's patience, especially if they are unfamiliar with their settings. But chances are that you won't have to mess with it on a regular schedule. Other cameras might have a separate ISO dial. Others may use the wheel to change these settings. No matter how many means you use, ISO still works at the same speed. All you need is to find out how to access ISO using your camera. This information will be in your owner's guide or user manual.

What can I do with ISO

What should you do now with all this information. ISO is not a setting you will change from one shot. For many cameras, the ISO setting is hidden behind the lens while the shutter speed/f stop options are visible. These are two sides of an exposure triangle you will use to fine tune your shot.

ISO is more a setting that you choose to use based on lighting conditions. When it comes to setting the ISO for a shot, getting familiar with your DSLR and its limitations is a great benefit. The more you practice with various ISO speeds, you'll be more comfortable using the lens.

ISO can be an easy element to forget when it involves photography. Yet, ISO is often overlooked or forgotten about. Shutter speed, aperture, and shutter speed, on the other hand, are well-known. This shouldn't happen. ISO is critical to creating stunning photography and ensuring that your DSLR is at its best. Do not underestimate the importance of setting ISO, it could easily make or ruin a shot.

Instead, focus on this part of the exposure triangle and put it to work in your photography. Understanding the purpose of ISO in photography is key to making the most of it. It can be useful if used with care. Without it, the exposure triangular would be devoid of one of its sizes. It would also mean that there is no chance for ever remaining evenly.

ISO can be intimidating at first. Take a deep dive and try it out. This is the only way you can truly learn about photography and other activities. The best way to overcome confusion is through practical experience. ISO is no different. It is possible to learn more about the intricacies of ISO.

Chapter 4: Opening Up About Aperture

What is Aperture, exactly?

Many photographers consider aperture (or "f stop") the most important element of the exposure Triangle. It's the small opening on your camera that lets in light when the shutter is open. Your eyes will shrink or dilate depending on how much sunlight is around. Your pupils expand when you enter dark rooms. These pupils dilate in order to see clearly in dimly lit environments. The aperture function is similar, but you have more control over the opening size, as it is not an autonomic function. You can adjust the aperture to suit your shooting conditions. When you take a picture, the aperture size will determine the exposure.

What Does Aperture Do?

The size of the aperture is the first thing that determines how light can enter. A smaller opening allows for less light to enter than one that is larger. This means that you can change the aperture size to alter the light entering. An aperture that is larger than the stop you are adding would be open, while one that is smaller would be closed.

The depth of field is also an effect produced by the aperture. The size of the aperture will influence the appearance of your shot as well as the tone.

A shallow depth in field is when the background or focus of your photo is not clear. The shallower your aperture is, the more your frame is out-of-focus. This is because lens aberrations can cause distortions. It is still possible to blur the background or foreground objects in order to highlight the subject. The subject of the shot will draw all your attention to what is in focus. Portraits can often be used with shallow depths of field, although not exclusively.

Deep depth is when every detail in your frame is clear, from your subject to the background. The deeper your aperture is, the more your frame is in focus. This will create a clear background and foreground, resulting in the clearest image. Landscape photography lends itself to deep depth of fields.

The effects of aperture can have other consequences, but we'll get to these later in this chapter. Aperture's main focus is on the amount of light and depth-of-field. The spectrum doesn't have to be the best, but it is possible that one side is more suitable for certain situations or preferences, depending on which shot you are taking.

What is F Stop, you ask?

F stop is the number you use to indicate how large your aperture is. It is commonly written as an equivalent to a fraction like f/11, F/8, and so forth. It can be complicated to figure out how the fstop number affects the size of an aperture. But shutter speed and fstops are actually fractions. The f/8 number is the same as the 1/11. However, f stop numbers progress slower than shutter speeds or ISOs. While these numbers are equally halved/doubled, the aperture employs a different set. While you can generally remember the chart, f stop are usually written on your lenses.

Different aperture effects can benefit from different fstops. For low light conditions, the best f stop is f/2.8. It allows more light into your camera sensor if you are in a darker area. f/2.8 is an excellent f stop for shallow depths of fields. This can also produce blurred background. An f stop closer than f/8, or f/11 will give you a sharper image if you want to shoot deep depth of fields.

Minimum and Maximum Perforations

Each lens will have an aperture minimum and maximum. The apertures that each lens can open or close will be limited. They will limit the size of the aperture opening that can be opened and what the maximum size can be. This limit can differ from lens to lens, as different lenses are meant for different types and types of photos.

Standard is f/16 with many lenses. This is adequate for taking everyday photos in standard lighting conditions. The minimum aperture is less important than maximum. The maximum aperture of your lens is the width at which it can open. This will determine how much light you will need for a good exposure. This is how dark your environment can get, and still be able to photograph.

Lenses are also identified by the speed of their minimum and maximum apertures. A fast lens will have a large aperture as f/1.4 or greater. This aperture allows light in and speeds up shutter speeds. These lenses are excellent for shooting indoors and in low light. A slow lens is one which has a smaller aperture than f/4. These lenses have slower shutter speeds, as they cannot let in as light as larger apertures.

Zoom lenses offer a completely different experience. We'll touch on them later. But, let us introduce the connection between aperture and zoom lenses here. The maximum fstop will change as you zoom in and/or out with your lens. However, it is usually the same minimum. The maximum aperture for zoom lens is usually f/2.8. It can change depending on whether you zoom in or outside at the time.

F Stop Specialties

Different f stops will be used for different shots. It is not an all-purpose tool, but more of a range. There are many options that can be used for all types of photography. There are many specialties that can overlap across ranges. However, these are great places to start if you want to capture various types of shots.

Sharpness is one of the main advantages of F stops in the range f/2.8 through f/4. F stops between 0.56 and 0.80 are excellent for shots of architecture and landscapes. There are many options for large-format photography. Photography from f/22 onwards is not recommended for beginners. Unless you have a good understanding of how to use these apertures, they can be dangerous. When using these apertures it is easy for sharpness to be lost quickly. Avoid these apertures until you're comfortable handling them.

Other Aperture Effects

While aperture is best known for affecting the brightness of your photos and the depth of field, there are many other effects your aperture can produce. These are important considerations to remember when shooting. This knowledge can come in handy if you encounter a block in your photography or discover an error in one of your shots. Your images could be saved by knowing the consequences of your aperture selection.

An aperture that is too small can cause reflection. Small apertures allow light to squeeze through. This results in poor quality images. Although diffraction will increase as your fstop decreases, it's not usually noticeable enough for it to be an issue. The aperture setting should not exceed f/11. But, diffraction may cause problems starting at f/22.

Lens aberrations can lead to poor image quality. They are not the result user error. However, lenses are not perfect. Each lens has its unique set of flaws. Some settings on your cameras can highlight these flaws. When lenses are made they have a tendency to have a sharper focus towards the center, and a slower decrease as you move towards its edges. This happens because creating lenses' centers is more challenging than creating them at their edges. An aperture that is smaller can eliminate this aberration, as the edges of the lens will be covered more often than the aperture. But, the bigger the aperture, however, the more aberrations are exposed. Be aware of this when choosing your aperture. The lens' edges can make subjects blurred and blurred as the aperture expands. If you don't check this, it can have negative effects on your image.

When using smaller apertures, you may experience focus shift. This aberration is caused by your focus shifting further back when you decrease your aperture. You can check for this flaw, which can pose a problem while shooting. The root of the problem is that lenses tend to be more sharp around the edges than they are at the centers. As your aperture shrinks your lens edges will cause problems with focus, they can also disrupt the focus of your shot.

Another flaw you could have with a small aperture is that it can highlight any specks or marks on your lens (or something else you are using like a window). An ordinary problem such as a drop of rain or specks dust can suddenly become a huge issue across your frame. Sometimes, you can just wipe your lens. Other times, it might require the help of a larger aperture.

Starbursts (or sun stars) are unique effects caused by light being partially blocked. You can get a stunning aesthetic from your photo by using smaller apertures. It's interesting to note that the number o the sun stars or starburst beams directly correlates with how many aperture blades your lens has. This number varies between lenses, so even if you're shooting in the same area, different lenses will produce different flares.

Similar to starbursts in that it deals with background blur caused by the size and shape of your aperture, bokeh can also be called blurred spots of light appearing in your background. These can be pleasingly aesthetically in a shot. They change shape based upon the shape and size of your aperture blades.

Finding the happy medium

There is no ideal solution for aperture or any other element in photography.

This brings us back the balance. When photographing, it is important that you find a happy medium. While every error can sometimes be wiped away, not every problem can ever be solved. We know that with the exposure triangle there will need be one element at the center, and that you may have to sacrifice some elements to achieve the best shot. Aperture is another example. Both too small and too large apertures have pros as well as cons. What should your shot be to look its best? Is it the small aperture? The larger one? Maybe an entirely different element? You, the photographer must decide what is most important when it comes aperture or any other element.

What do you do with your Aperture?

All this information is important to remember, so you might be wondering where to start in the process of aperture. The best way to answer this question is to take each step one at a time. Aperture is a key factor in determining the quality of your photos. The practice of aperture will help you achieve anything beyond these limits. Although you can explore the effects listed above further, it's okay to start from scratch. Like any successful dive in an artform, expertise and improvement take time. Be open to learning and enjoy the experience of photography.

Chapter 5: Shutter Speed – The Hare And The Tortoise

What is Shutter Speed exactly?

Shutter speed may seem complicated but it is easy to explain. Shutter speed simply refers to how long your shutter is open before you take a picture or the speed at the shutter closes. The shutter captures the photo when it is open. Shutter speed controls the brightness as well the sharpness and blurred motion of the camera. The rest of the chapter will discuss this. The shutter speed will determine how you want your action to appear in the frame. While aperture is determined by depth of field, it is also determined by how wide you want it. A shot that requires shutter speed and aperture to be your priority must have both. Each adjustment will change the photo. In these cases, only one element is allowed to have its way. It is you, the photographer who must decide.

The shutter covers the sensor in a DSLR. It controls the shutter's speed, which determines how light reaches the sensor. This affects the quality of the image. While you cannot change shutter speed in auto mode (or in shutter priority), you can do so in manual or shutter priority modes. You have two options for controlling shutter speed. Manual mode will give you the most control, allowing you to mix and match shutter speeds to get the best shot.

The speed at which you set the shutter speed depends on what kind of light you are using. Low light conditions require slower shutter speeds in order to properly expose the photograph. You need to allow light into your sensor in order to capture the photo. A faster shutter speed is required for brighter environments.

The appropriate amount of light must be allowed in order to expose it. You must remember that shutter speeds can differ depending on what settings you have in your camera. The balance act is what matters, even though these principles will always apply.

Measurement

Shutter speed may be measured in seconds or fractions of seconds. A DSLR will display the shutter speed in fractions.

The screen only displays the denominator of the fraction. The display indicates 1" or higher when the shutter speed reaches one second. It depends on how much time the shutter is opened. The quotation mark is used to indicate that the number displayed takes place over a full second. Any number without a quote mark is a fractional part of a second.

Many DSLRs have speeds of 1/4000 to 1/8000. Many can be set-up to allow for a thirty-second exposure. However, this is possible without the use of bulb mode. Some cameras let you shoot at third stop increments. Others do not.

Frozen Action Vs. Motion Blur

It is crucial to remember what kind of shot your goal is when you choose a shutterspeed. What kind of motion is happening on the other end of the lens Is it moving quickly? How quickly? Are the subjects moving at a rapid pace? The shutter speed can be used to decide if the action will be blurred or froze in the shot. Each option has a unique aesthetic that can be used for different shots. You can also achieve different settings. Both of these possibilities can be achieved with a DSLR. These options and how to choose each will be discussed next. Let's start with fast shutter speeds.

Rapid Exposure

Fast shutter speeds can allow less light to enter the sensor when you expose. It is recommended to use this speed when shooting in bright surroundings or when you wish to freeze action. Fast shutter speeds are the key to many amazing still-action shots.

Your speed of photography will depend on how fast your subject is moving. The speed at which the subject is moving will dictate the speed at the pace you need to capture it. These speeds are usually used for shooting sports events. Shooting running water at a fast shutter speed allows you to see individual droplets and rivulets within the final shot. Fast shutter speeds can also be used to capture wildlife. If taken correctly, all these shots will produce stunning results.

Fast speeds can range from 1/1000 of seconds to 1/200 or even 1/1000 of a sec before you get camera shake. Camera shake, as mentioned above, occurs when the shutter speed becomes slow enough to record your hand movements even while you are standing still. This shake could blur your shot and ruin it.

Fast shutter speeds can be used to freeze moments in time. These photos show the viewer the incredible moments that occurred both before the shutter was released and afterwards. Consider a sports shot. A basketball player is in midair dribbling the ball. A fast shutter speed would freeze the moment in time. This would remove any motion blur and only show the image of the athlete in flight. Another example would also be the one of a waterfall. You can take two images of the exact same waterfall using different shutter speeds. The opposite effect could occur. We'll cover the slow shutter speeds effect later. However, for now, we'll stick with the quick. This waterfall would freeze in an instant if you used a fast shutter speed. The frame would show droplets of spray and water that were crisp and clean. The waterfall's power would hang heavy in the air, and the image would be strong. The image may seem still, but there is the promise and reality of the rushing water below. These are just some examples of the effects that a quick shutter speed can produce.

Slow exposure

Slow shutter speeds enable the shutter to remain open for longer time periods, which allows more light through. Slower shutter speeds require a tripod to prevent camera shake from ruining the shot. Many lenses do not allow slow shutter speeds and require a tripod. But, blurring your image is one of the goals of this speed. However, it will only blur the subject in motion and leave the rest crisp. These speeds will blur anything that is moving in the shot.

This shot is often used to highlight speed or motion. Slower shutter speeds can be used to photograph moving cars and running water if you wish for a soft, blurred effect. A slow shutter speed shot usually requires a long exposure of more than 1 second.

Let's imagine the types of shots that benefit from slow shutter speeds. Picture the car moving through the frame. If we use a slow shutter speed, it would be difficult to see details of this car. Or all of them. This type shot would aim to highlight the speed and movement of the subject. While the photo depicts a moment in time we should remember that the subject moves at all times. If the photographer didn't capture it with a camera, it would disappear in a second. Let's revisit our waterfall shot.

With a fast shutter speed, all the details of this powerful, majestic water were displayed. A slower shutter speed will result in a different shot. The blurred water will appear in the frame as the shutter speed slows down, while the scene surrounding it will still be sharp. This photo would show a completely different emotion. These are just some of the effects you could expect from slow shutter speeds.

The Reciprocal rule

The reciprocal principle is an equation that can determine the slowest shutter speed possible with any lens without experiencing blurred images or camera shake. This equation is made by multiplying focal length (the measurement indicated on the lens) times the camera crop factor. Next, multiply that number by the camera's crop factor. That gives you a fraction. This is the slowest shutter speed that your camera can be set to without creating motion blur. This only applies to steady holding of the camera. This means that you can determine how your camera reacts to motion blur and camera shake. Keeping the camera steady is key.

Other shutter speed modes

Apart from manual mode and shutter priority there are several other modes for your DSLR. These modes allow you different settings for the shutter speed, so that you can achieve the desired effect. These modes can be used to alter shutter speed and produce different effects, such as time, bulb, x200 and x250.

Bulb Mode

Bulb mode can be used on your DSLR to allow you to hold down your shutter button and capture your photo for as long time as you like. To keep the shutter open, hold down the button and the light will continue to enter the camera for as long that you are pressing the button. Photographers often use shutter release cables to help ensure the button is securely held. Shutter cable cables can also be used to avoid camera shakes that may occur when pressing the button long enough.

You can use the bulb mode to create many different shots. This is the easiest way to paint with light. If you hold the shutter open in dark environments, any light will show up as light trails. This effect is used by many photographers to create stunning pieces using just such light trails. This effect can produce a unique and beautiful look. The more movement captured in the shot the better. Use bulb mode with care to achieve stunning and sophisticated results.

Bulb mode also allows for time-lapse shots. Any object that moves across the frame with the shutter open will trail across your shot. In some cases, this can give the illusion of speed. This effect is most evident when shooting stars. If you take long exposures of the stars, they will leave trails in the sky. They are being dragged along the earth's spin. While it's not always what you want when photographing the night skies, it can be very beautiful when captured properly.

Time Mode

Time mode is very like bulb mode. The shutter can be left open for however long you wish, often longer than shutter priority mode or manual. There is one difference between time mode and bulb mode. In time mode you press the shutter key to open the shutter. To close it, you then press it again. This mode is very handy as it allows you to not have to hold the shutter open while you are using your camera. This mode is not present on all cameras. It is a rare feature that you can take advantage of if you have it.

X200, x250, Etc.

These modes allow you match your shutter speed to the flash sync rate. This is how fast you can set your shutterspeed and still use a flash. This mode isn't the most groundbreaking, as it's similar to setting your shutter speed up to 1/200 or 1/250th of a second. But, if this mode is useful to you, you can use this mode as a quick way to change your flash sync speeds on your camera. This mode doesn't require you to be able to flash at all, so you don't need to keep track of what your shutter speed should be. The camera will take care.

Shutter Speed: What is it important?

Shutter speed should be one of your most important settings. Depending on the type or shot you want, the shutter speed should be set first, before setting aperture and other settings.

Shutter speed dictates what type shot you end with, regardless of whether there is any movement in the frame. It is important to consider shutter speed when shooting water, wildlife, and other natural subjects. When you shoot any of these things, you will first need to decide what shutter speed is required. Do you want the subject to be frozen in motion? Do you want to blur the action? First, this will tell you how fast or slow the shutter speed must be to capture your desired shot. Now you will only need to adjust the settings of the camera to match the shutter speed. Make the shutter speed your priority if you want to capture motion.

Chapter 6: Choosing Your Own Body

There are many types

If you're just starting out as a photographer, or any photographer for that matter, you will need to pick the type of camera that you want. There are many models to choose from. We will focus on three of them: DSLRs and DSLRs. Each has its own pros/cons and uses, depending on the purpose of your photography.

Before you make your decision, get familiar with each camera model and consider what kind and style of photography you'd like to pursue. These points will help to determine which camera body best suits your preferences.

It is possible that you want to learn more about DSLRs if you're reading this. This chapter will discuss three types of cameras, but will be focused on the DSLR. The two other types of bodies that we will cover can be useful but only get you so far in photography.

Compact Cameras

Compact cameras are among the most basic of all the body types. They are also known as point and shoot cameras. This is because they allow you to use them in a simple way. They were created for photographers to be simple to use. All settings can be controlled by the camera. The person behind the lens is only responsible for pointing out and shooting. Although they moved to digital with time, the point and shoot has remained. They are the ideal camera to capture every moment. You can use them anywhere you wish. As with all cameras, they come with their pros as well as cons.

Compact Cameras Have Their Pros

Cameras aside, compact cameras can produce better photos than the ones on most phones. Camera phones don't have the same quality sensors, so they are attractive for day to-to-day photography.

The compact camera also has zoom lenses and meters, which can be used for exposure. These functions are done automatically. They have all the settings they need, including focus. Additionally, presets are available for specific shooting situations such as landscape and portraiture. A compact camera is a great choice for those who do not want complete control but still want photos that are specifically tailored for different shooting situations.

Compact cameras are also affordable, which is one of their many benefits. If you're not looking for a camera that will take great photos, compact cameras may be a good choice. Cameras that can take care most of the elements for each shot are cheaper.

The fact that they are lightweight and portable makes them great for traveling. Many models can be carried in your pocket and have wrist straps for safety and convenience while you shoot.

Cons of Compact Cameras

A compact camera is convenient but not a professional camera. Be aware of this when purchasing a compact camcorder. The settings are mostly taken care off by the software, so the person in front of the lens doesn't have much control. These cameras can be described as point-and shot. You cannot adjust ISO, aperture, or shutter speeds by yourself. The camera does that for you. You do not have much control over composition.

While compact cameras may not offer the highest resolution, they can easily surpass phones' cameras.

Compact cameras come with a viewfinder which allows you to see the image. Viewfinders can show the image side-by-side, but are higher than the lens so they may not provide the most accurate rendering. Due to the fact that you may not see the lens, the photos may not look exactly how you intended.

Bridge Cameras

Bridge cameras bridge that gap between DSLRs/compact cameras. They are small and light, but they can also be battery-powered and have a fixed focal length. Although bridge cameras are more capable of taking better photos than compact ones, they still fall behind DSLRs. While they provide a better quality image than compact cameras, bridge cameras are not recommended for advanced photographers. However, they can be used to take photos at a basic level.

Bridge Cameras: Pros and Cons

Bridge cameras can be used as a bridge camera, which is somewhere in the middle of compact cameras and DSLRs. Their larger sensors allow for better quality shots. A DSLR is more difficult to use, but they are still very easy to use. Fixed zoom lenses on bridge cameras offer a range of options. These cameras make an excellent in-between camera and provide better quality than compact cameras. They also offer slightly more control but don't sacrifice the ease of use that point & shoot cameras are known for.

Cons of Bridge Cameras

Although the bridge cameras are an improvement on compact cameras, they don't offer the same benefits and features as DSLRs. While not terrible, the quality of photos taken by bridge cameras is inferior to those captured with DSLRs. Bridge cameras are also difficult to control, and they have a bad reputation for low battery life. Additionally, bridge cameras have lenses that are less high quality than professional or higher-quality models.

DSLR Cameras

DSLR (or Digital Single Lens Reflex), cameras are the central focus. These are the best choices for photographers looking to start photography or improve their skills. DSLRs have the greatest control and customization capabilities. The most diverse cameras that we will be covering, they come in a range of price points from the lowest end to the highest. While they are heavier than most other camera bodies, they are still durable and can be taken with you. DSLRs are the best option if you want to learn more and make progress in the field.

DSLRs' Pros

DSLRs offer many advantages. DSLRs offer more control and creativity than any other camera type, while DSLRs only offer manual mode. Additionally, they offer manual mode as well as automatic mode. This allows for photographers of all levels and many preferences. The DSLR has many more benefits.

DSLRs have a wide range of interchangeable lens options to allow you to shoot in different situations. These will be covered more in the next section. However, it is important for you to understand that DSLRs are able to use all types and lenses. This gives you the greatest variety when it comes to the photo type you wish to take. With a DSLR, you can use a macro lens and zoom lens. Prices of these lenses vary depending on what kind of lens you require and how much you want to spend. While some lenses might be more expensive, they are an investment in the art of photography and even a career.

It is important that you consider the available sensors when selecting a DSLR. Your images' quality will depend on how big these sensors are. DSLRs have smaller sensors than other camera types.

A DSLR also has an internal benefit in the form of its viewfinder. A DSLR has an optical viewfinder. This uses both a mirror and a prism to show the photo upside down and through the lens. This provides the best image view before you even take the shot without any compromises in convenience. The shutter is pressed and the mirror flips up, revealing the sensor.

Additionally, DSLRs can use battery packs. This rechargeable battery allows you to extend your shoot by swapping out a dying battery for a new one and cycling along. The battery won't die and you will be able to continue shooting. Other cameras may require you to charge the battery or replace it. However, a DSLR can be used to change out the dead batteries for a charged one. Then you can charge the battery and make it ready for the next use. While this may mean that you need to buy more batteries, it is worth it. It can also save you time and money when you have backups.

Cons of DSLR Cameras

DSLR cameras may have many great features, but they aren't the right choice for all photographers. The most important downside is the price. DSLRs are one of the most expensive options that we have reviewed, but they come in a range of prices from moderately affordable to very high. Also, lenses are often more expensive than their bodies. It is possible to need multiple lenses depending upon the type of photography. You might also have to add customization. These add-ons include external flash or flash gear, shutter release cables, filter and so forth. Each component serves a purpose and can make stunning images. However, these add-ons can cost quite a bit.

DSLRs are also bulkier than most other cameras. This makes it difficult to have them with you at all times. They cannot be carried in your pocket, or hang from your wrist. Their bodies are weather-sealed to protect them in all shooting environments.

Final, DSLRs offer the best learning curve out of all the cameras. DSLRs can be used in a more intuitive way than bridge cameras and point-and–shoots. However, DSLRs require more work and patience to properly use to create stunning images. Although this may seem intimidating to beginners, it is possible to make great photos with the right practice. You can produce stunning photos by yourself, even if you are unable to use the same tools as others.

How to Select a Camera Body

Ultimately, what you want the most from your camera is what determines which camera body you choose. Compact and bridge cameras provide experience in composition but do not allow for creative expression beyond that. The photographer is more controlled by their surroundings and subject to what the camera thinks will produce the best exposure. This level of control may be all that some photographers desire or need from their camera. Perhaps you simply want a compact camera that can be used to quickly capture memories and moments during the day or on family road trips. These compact cameras, as well as bridge cameras, would be ideal.

These are just a starting point in the worlds of photography. If you are looking to advance beyond the beginner stage, then the DSLR is for you. It is the best camera system available to those who really want to learn photography.

If so, you might want to start searching for your DSLR. Canon and Nikon, two of the biggest names within photography, are likely ones you've heard. You can find other good DSLRs made by other companies, but these two are the most popular. Both are wonderful choices when it comes to purchasing a DSLR. As technology evolves, you can easily swap out your camera body for the latest features. You can also keep your expensive lenses. It's a wise investment for budget because cameras bodies tend to be significantly cheaper than lenses. This is a fantastic way to keep up with the latest technology without breaking the bank every time it comes out.

The last chapter of the book will provide additional information about the various lenses available for DSLRs. This information enhances the versatility of a DSLR camera and gives a clear picture of why this camera is the best choice to help beginners get started in the art of photography.

Chapter 7: The Holy Trinity And Prime Lenses

Introduction to DSLR Lenses

DSLR cameras are equipped with interchangeable lenses, which affects the variety of photos you can shoot. You can mount multiple lenses to your camera, or just one body. This depends on what kind of shoot you're doing. For starters, what exactly is a Lens?

Lenses are a set of glass plates that have been placed inside a tube, and then mounted to a body. The lens is able to focus light on the sensor of the camera by taking in light. This collection of light creates the image.

How the light rays collide with a lens is called focus. This is where the focus will be. This can be done with manual focus lenses. The actions are not affected by the way the photographer interacts with them. Manually focusing a lens allows you select a specific subject or portion of a topic to keep crisp. Depending upon the type of lens used and how precise you need it to be, focus can prove difficult. Still, manipulating focus can add a lot to an image's depth, drawing the viewer in wherever the photographer wishes. This skill is vital for your photographic prowess.

Focal Length

The focal length (or distance) of a lens refers to how far the lens is from its subject. A lens has a focal length that is determined by the distance between the light source and the lens. This is called "the nodal" point. The focal distance of the lens is measured from this point to the sensor. It is most commonly measured in millimeters.

The focal length can determine what kind of shot the lens will take as well as the magnification. Magnifying the image with a longer focal length will magnify it. Images that are shorter than this focal length can be magnified by larger angles. Different types are best for different types of photos and use different focal lengths. The details will be covered in the next chapter when we discuss the three prime lense we will cover.

Lens Versatility

DSLR lenses improve the versatility of any camera you purchase, since you have complete control over what type of image you capture.

It is important to note that lenses come in different sizes and brands. Some lenses are different. A lens is not interchangeable beyond its brand. There are adapters, which let you attach a Nikon lens onto a Canon body. There are many options. It is common to mix and match lenses or bodies. This allows for creativity and individualization. Every shot calls for a different combination. Being able choose the best lens combination and the body that is most appropriate for each shot will help you grow as a professional photographer.

There are many options for lens types, but we won't cover all of them. Our goal is just to get you started in DSLR photography. This chapter will focus on three major types of lenses, the prime lens.

Prime Lenses

Prime lenses can be used as a type of DSLR lens. Each has a fixed focal-length, which means that you cannot zoom in/out with them. Although it may seem annoying, the fixed focal lengths of lenses offer many advantages in terms both of their quality and abilities as well as the practice they give photographers. Moving your body to change the distance, angle and composition of a prime lenses is necessary. The lens will not allow you to do this. This is a good practice because it forces the photographer take the time to examine every part of the shot. To find the perfect shot, the photographer should intentionally alter any element that doesn't feel right. Some zoom lenses, such as the Zoom lens, can cause too much trouble for photographers. This is why they need to be able to fix every issue in their photos from a stationary position. Photographing hands-on is always a good idea.

Prime lenses produce sharper images due to their fixed focal length. Prime lenses are lighter than many other types and therefore are easier to carry. This is great for when you need to have more than one lens, depending on your shooting environment and what kind of shot you are taking. Because prime lenses are lightweight, they can be carried easily on the go.

Prime lenses make a great starting point for gathering equipment to support your photographic endeavors. Even if your goal is to become a professional photographer, you should have at least one lens to start with. These will provide both a solid foundation as well a place to expand. The trio of prime lenses, which are the three types of lens that make up the Trinity of Prime Lenses, provide many options for beginning photographers.

50mm Lenses

The 50mm lens, also called the "Nifty Fifty", can be a great place for beginners to start when purchasing lenses. 50 mm refers the focal length of a lens. It is a normal size that provides a standard view. So, out of all three types of lenses, the 50mm captures a picture that is closest to the one we can see with our eyes. There is no pulling or stretching the background or subject. This lens doesn't magnify, close in or shrink the subject. The 50mm lens allows you to see the subject in the best possible light. In essence, you see what you get.

One advantage to the 50mm focal length lens is its large maximum apertures. Most lenses of this length offer an aperture range from f/2.8 to f/1.2. These apertures enable shallow depths of field. A shallow depth in field is one where the subject appears sharp while the background becomes blurred. Although the 50mm lens has less blur than the larger 35mm, the background can still be seen. This lens can be used in a way that creates a pleasant aesthetic.

The 50mm lens also has large apertures which allow light to enter the lens, allowing for fast shutter speeds even in low light situations. These lenses eliminate blurring and camera shake. This is especially useful when you don't have any tripod and are shooting in dark conditions.

This shutter speed advantage allows for you to capture the stars as it appears, and not as trails as previously mentioned. The spinning earth is not an issue when you try to capture the stars because you can get below twenty-five second at night using a 50mm zoom lens. The stars appear as lines in the final shot because of the earth's movement. However, this is due to the fact that the typical shutter speeds for such a light environment are not fast enough to keep up with the rotation. A 50mm lens is able to overcome this problem, and allows the photographer the freedom to take pictures at a speed fast sufficient to capture the stars.

50mm lenses offer versatility and are a great starting lens for photographers. Because they are the middle of three prime lenses, they are able to capture a variety of shots. You can think of portrait photography as a way to see what you can get from a 50mm zoom lens. These lenses are a happy compromise. They offer the ability to take simple photos while also offering a variety of benefits that can't be found with other lenses. The background may be blurred if you are shooting close enough to the subject. However, it will not be too distracting. The 50mm lens is wide enough to allow for full-body shots. The background cannot be altered so that the eye is attracted to the entire image and not to the subject.

The standard 50mm lens, which is not a macro or wide lens (both of them will be covered), captures the most true to life images of the three. Perfect for daily photography.

35mm Lenses

The 35mm lens has been described as a wide-angle lens. It also has its advantages and uses just like its two predecessors. Another great beginner lens, 35mm, can be used to capture shots like landscape, architecture, and street photos. Many beginners photographers know the style and image that this lens creates. It's very similar in appearance to the default setting on their iPhone cameras. This lens will make the background appear smaller in your final image. A wide-angle lens allows more foreground to be included in the final image.

This lens is ideal for candid photography. While it creates a lovely aesthetic, it is less accurate than the 50 mm. The 35mm lens has its own uses. This distortion can also be used creatively. It is attractive for landscape photography, street photography and architecture. The background of a 35mm lens is better for highlighting the subject, as it provides less distraction. When the background is reduced and the foreground expanded, your eyes will naturally be drawn to what you are photographing. Let's be more specific about portrait photography. A 35mm lens may cause distortions that can be beneficial to the photographer, but it's not always an advantage when it comes portrait photography. The distortion caused by the 35mm lens's foreground stretching causes close-ups to be inaccurate and the person is unable to be recognized. This is not intended to be a criticism about the 35mm. However, it does show the effect the lens has on an image. For larger images, such like landscapes, 35mm lenses will produce the same results as the portraits.

Maximum aperture for 35mm lenses is f/4. There are also lenses that can be adjusted to f/2.8. However, these are generally more expensive. In addition, the more expensive the lens, you will experience less distortion, which in turn makes the shots closer to reality. Even though 35mms can be more expensive, they still do a good job and are worth the price. They would not be among the three most highly recommended prime lenses.

85mm Lenses

85mm lenses can also be called macro lenses. Because of their ability to capture macro images and close-ups, macro lenses are well-suited. You can get stunning images of even the smallest things with this lens. 85mm lenses can be used to capture stunning close-ups. Imagine a large-thanlife image of a droplet dripping onto a blade of grass or the strings that make up a spider's web. These extraordinary images are made possible by using a macro-lens.

These are just some of the types of shots that an 85mm lens can capture. They are also great for portraits. They maintain more exact proportions than a standard 35mm lens. 85mm lenses draw your eye closer to the subject and make the background appear more three-dimensional. These effects help reduce distractions in the photo and focus the subject.

85mm lenses generally have an aperture limit of f/2.8. The shallow depth of the field makes it tricky to focus but is also important. It can be difficult to focus on a larger subject, or group of subjects, without letting anything blur. The end result can be very satisfying when you get the focus right.

Prime Lenses: Get Started

These three prime lenses, which are discussed in Chapter 1, make an excellent starting kit for your collection. The trinity is a good starting point for beginner photographers, even though you may not be able to purchase them all at once.

Start with the 50mm. Then, go further. The 50mm lens is versatile and can be used for a variety shots. It will also help you become familiar with the art of photographing. The 50mm lens will give you a solid foundation in DSLR photography thanks to its consistent use and precise approach to capturing images. From there, choose the type of photography that you would like to do next. Is it time to zoom out, or zoom in, from the 50 mm's basic shots? Are you ready to zoom in or out? Or will it be a trip to the smallest of wonders that allows you to look at them from a different perspective and allow the world to see them?

Your lens will help you tell a tale with photography. What kind of story do your want to tell, and what lens will you use? This trinity, which ranges from 50mm through 85mm, can help you tell a different story every day. The possibilities are endless.

Chapter 8: Steps On How To Use Your Dslr Camera

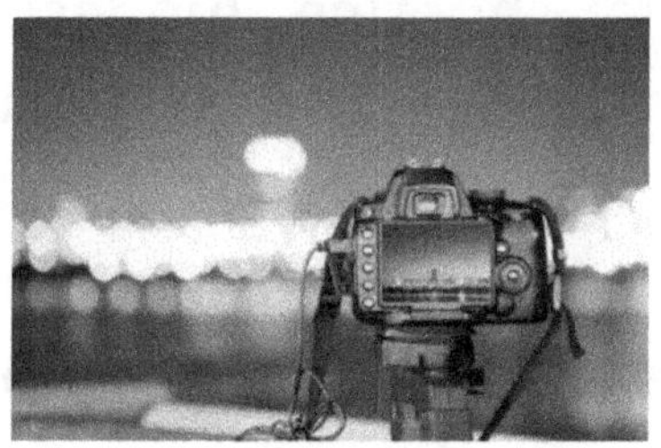

Either you are contemplating buying a DSLR for the first time or you already have one, it is important to understand many things. These are just some examples:
* Shooting Modes
* Understanding ISO
* Exposure Triangle
* Exposure Compensation and Metering
* File Size and Type

* White Balance

Step 1 Learn the Shooting Methods

The shooting modes are the most important thing to learn when using a DSLR. The shooting modes can be found on the camera's top with a dial labeled Auto, Tv., M., Av., and Pa. Your camera's settings will be affected by the mode selected when you press the shutter. By choosing "Auto", your camera will automatically adjust exposure, shutter speed, as well as aperture speed.

You may be thinking that my DSLR has a dial mode different to other DSLRs. But this isn't something you should be worried about. Different manufacturers use different labeling systems. For example, Av and P and M might be replaced with Tv and M. You may instead get A, P and M and S. All of them work in the exact same way. To ensure this, you can refer to the manual or product guide provided by your manufacturer.

What are these modes, then?

Aperture priority A or Av

This mode can also be called semi-automatic. You only have to set your aperture. Your camera will automatically select the shutter speed when you choose this mode. Accordingly, aperture is the size of a lens opening that allows light to pass through when the shutter opens. In other words, light will flow through larger apertures.

The aperture is usually measured in F-stops. Therefore, an fnumber (which translates to the ratio focal length/opening diameter) is used to display the aperture. The f-number of a larger aperture will be lower. The opposite happens. A smaller aperture means a bigger f-number. The amount light that enters the camera is reduced by one f stop.

Photography is dependent on the aperture, which has a significant impact on the "depth" of field. The aperture also has a direct impact on the amount of focus in an image. If the depth is large, it means there is a lot of space in the scene that is in focus. A shallow depth of fields will reveal an image with a sharply focused subject and a background that is soft. This feature is often used when you want to shoot portraiture or wildlife. Using aperture priority also gives you the ability to adjust the depth of focus and let the camera do the rest.

Shutter Priority - TV or S

Similar to the aperture preference, the shutter priority can also be used semi-automatically. In this instance, the shutter speed is controlled by the photographer and the aperture is managed by the camera. The shutter speed refers in seconds to the time the shutter stays open during a snap.

This is because more light passes through an aperture to the sensor, if it stays open longer.

You will need to choose a shorter shutter speed if you plan on freezing a fast-moving object. Photographing moving animals or racing cars is one example. Your tripod will help you keep the shutter open steady. But, if blurring an object in motion, such as a waterfall for example, you should use longer shutter speeds. When using a Tv/S mode, you can adjust the shutter speed, while the camera sets the aperture to achieve the desired exposure.

Program (P).

This mode is approximately halfway between semiautomatic control and full manual. This mode allows the user to set the aperture and shutter speed. The camera will maintain the correct exposure by making adjustments to one of the settings. This means that if the aperture is changed, the shutter speed will be adjusted automatically. The shutter priority and aperture priority offer additional freedom without the need to switch between them.

Manual (M).

The manual mode gives you full control of the exposure, setting the shutter speed, and priority. In this instance, the exposure indicator, visible on the screen or in the viewfinder, tells you whether the image was under- or overexposed. You have the option to adjust the shutter speed and aperture to ensure the correct exposure.

Tip 1: Take your camera out of auto mode to learn how to use it. This is because shutter priority and aperture are the two most important settings that can be used to help you understand how your DSLR settings affect your images.

Step 2 Understanding the ISO

ISO is the ISO number that indicates the camera's light sensitivity. This term came from film photography. Films of different sensitivities were used to determine the shooting conditions. ISO 100 can be described numerically. It represents low sensitivity through ISO 6400. ISO 6400 above is high sensitivity. It controls the amount light that the camera's sensor needs to achieve the correct exposure. Sensitivity is a measure of how much light is required to create the desired exposure. High sensitivity, however, requires less light to achieve desired exposure. Let's talk about the differences in ISO numbers between low ISO and high ISO numbers.

High ISO numbers

It is frequently used when shooting in low light conditions (e.g., dark rooms where not much light is available). The sensor's sensitivity increases when the

ISO number is very high (e.g. ISO 3200). The camera allows light to multiply so that the image is properly exposed.

However, an ISO of very high quality could result in images with less detail due to higher noise. This could cause images to look grainy. This effect becomes more prominent as the room darkens and there are shadows.

Low ISO numbers

It is usually used outdoors when there's plenty of light available for exposure. Also, the sensor doesn't need be very sensitive to obtain the right exposure. ISO 100 is recommended for high-quality images. Tip - Keep the ISO number to a minimum. This is because lower ISO numbers result in less noise which will produce high-quality images. Try a lower ISO number when you go out on sunny days. A lower ISO number is recommended for sunny days. As you move indoors, increase your ISO number to approximately 1600.

The good news is that almost all DSLR cameras now have an Auto-ISO function. This allows to adjust the ISO of your camera based on the amount light available, so that you can keep the ISO at its lowest setting. Auto-ISO, which allows you limit the maximum ISO setting for your camera's first use, is important.

Step 3 Learn the Exposure Triangle

The exposure triangle is composed of shutter speed, ISO, and aperture. All of them work together to control light through the camera and achieve the right exposure.

To control your DSLR better, you will need to know how these parts interact. Keep in mind that each setting affects the other. An example: If you lower the depth, but choose to use an aperture that is f/5.0, the aperture will increase, increasing light penetration. In order to achieve a balanced exposure, you could reduce the shutter speed by one factor or decrease the ISO by another factor.

This means that all of these factors have the combined effect of reducing light entering the camera. It also counters the aperture change. Understanding the interdependence between these three factors is key. If one of them changes, it will affect the other.

A combination of semi-automatic and ISO modes does not mean that you have to adjust exposure first. Understanding the relationship between ISO, aperture, and shutter speed is a first step towards mastering how to use your DSLR.

Step 4: Master the Measurement

We have already mentioned that the exposure is calculated using the amount of sunlight. You need to be able to understand what your DSLR is doing.

The camera calculates the average exposure automatically when taking a photo. To put it another way, the camera will try to determine the exposure by looking at both the darker and lighter areas. This is vital to ensure that all images have an average of 18% grey.

Metering refers to this step. Metering is the reason why an image taken from a bright white background will always appear darker than the original. It is the same with taking photos of dark scenes.

The main reason is that the camera is automatically averaging the scene. In many cases, this creates an image that looks correctly exposed. It is possible to control the scenes being assessed by your camera, so it can influence the way that the exposure is metered.

There are 3 types of metering methods. The following:

Spot Metering

This refers a situation in a scene where the camera only has access to a very small area. In most cases it is a circle at the centre of the viewfinder, which makes up around 5%. It evaluates the dark tones in the area. Then it exposes the entire scene, beginning with the assessment, to around 18% gray.

Average

In this example, the camera will examine the whole scene's tones starting from the corners and then expose the scene up to about 18% of that assessment.

Center-Weighted

This mode uses the camera's exposure reading to determine the percentage of the scene that is in the middle of its viewfinder. In this case, however the corner is ignored.

Tip. When you first start using your DSLR camera, the average and the middle-weighted center-weighted Metering Modes are the best starting points. This is because they provide a consistent measure to expose the scene. If you only choose one mode, stick with it. This helps you understand why a scene may appear different to the way it looks with your naked eye.

The main question is "What do I do in case the area is underexposed/overexposed?"

Exposure compensation can be used to compensate for the loss of light. This can be found on the shutter's small +/- button. It is one of the most important functions for anyone who wants to learn how to use a DSLR. It lets you adjust the default reading on your camera's meter to adjust the scene's brightness.

This means that if a scene contains bright tones and is being rendered dark by the camera, you can apply positive Exposure Compensation to it. It will tell the camera that the scene should be lighter than middle grey.

Negative exposure compensation can be used to correct for scenes that are primarily dark or being rendered light.

Step 5: How to Focus

It doesn't really make a difference what ISO setting or camera mode you use. The chances are there will be one subject that you are most interested in focusing on. If you don't achieve this focus, the image won't look exactly like what you want.

Some focus modes you should be familiar with include:

Autofocus modes

Noting that DSLRs are available in a wide range autofocus modes, it is important to remember. The most important are AF C or AF.

AF-C

AF-C stands for autofocus-continuous. This function is especially useful for taking photos of objects in motion/action, like wildlife and sports. Once you have pressed the shutter halfway to acquire the focus, it locks onto a specific subject. If the subject moves, then the focus will adjust with it. This means it will keep refining until the photo has been taken.

AF-S

It stands for "autofocus-single". It is best for stationary objects such people, buildings or landscapes to be photographed. By pressing the shutter halfway the focus is automatically acquired. The button must be held down for the rest of the time. To change the focus you can release the button, press halfway, and recompose.

Caution! You need to be able to distinguish between these and the other AF/MF switches that are found on the lens. MF stands in manual focus. AF simply stands out for autofocus. You can switch between manual and autofocus on your lens.

Focus points

These modes depend on the focal points. If you view the scene through a viewfinder, then you must be able to see the number or squares overlaid. If you press the shutter halfway on your camera, you should see one of these squares highlighted red. This is your current focus point. The camera focuses on this spot within the frame.

A new DSLR will have over 50 focus point. Many are tempted by this high number to focus their attention on auto focus point selection. You must remember that you alone know what focus you are trying to put your attention on. Focusing on the right subject is more important than having a single focus.

By selecting a single focus spot, you should easily be able to switch the active point using one of directional buttons. Alternately, choosing a focus point on your intended subject will ensure that the lens focuses exactly where it should. After several practice sessions, it will become easier for you to change focus without needing to remove the camera from your eye.

Tip: Set your camera first to a single point of focus. This allows you to focus on the desired subject and will ensure you get the best possible shot. Once you've mastered the basics of the various focus modes and how to select the focus point, it will be easy to move on to more advanced modes.

Step 6 Understanding the differences in file sizes.

The DSLR camera has the ability to change the file type as well as the size of each image. The maximum file size that the camera can record is recommended. This allows you to get the most out the number of megapixels you have.

You can choose whether to save your images in RAW and jpeg. It will either keep the image data uncompressed so that the file contains more information, which allows for more flexibility during post-processing, OR it will take it as jpeg. Jpeg is a compressed file format that the camera automatically processes. The great thing about this is that it will produce a print-ready picture straight from the camera. These images are smaller than files. You can therefore fit as many images to your memory cards as you want.

Tip 1: Jpeg makes it easy to start with your DSLR. This allows you get the best results as your camera continues to improve.

Step 7: Learn more about White Balance

If you shoot in Jpeg, make sure you set the white balance before you take the picture. Your photos will be corrected by the white balance. You may have noticed a blueish hue in some images and orange in others. This is the effect of the white balance. Although it is possible to adjust the image of your computer to improve it, it is easier to start from scratch.

This is due to the fact that there are many light sources available, including sunlight, bulb light, and fluorescent stripe. Because these light sources emit light at different wavelengths, there is a wide variety in color temperatures. For instance, light from the sun or a candle can be very warm and have a red-orange wavelength. The brain recognizes this kind of colored light and will reflect it off the surface to counter the effect. This means that you will be able to see the white surfaces as they are.

However, the DSLR camera is not able to function unless told so. This means that even if the surface has a certain color, such as orange, red, or blue, the camera can't correct it.

A second important point to be aware of is the fact that many color temperatures exist. To help with this effect, presets are available to your camera. The main goal is to capture the correct colors. The AWB auto feature will simply detect the scene's predominant color, then counter it. However, there are times when the camera cannot make the correct decision. In these cases, you may end up with incorrect colors. To avoid any mishaps, ensure that you set the color balance for your DSLR before taking any photographs. This includes the following.

Daylight setting is to be used for clear sunny days. This is because bright sunlight on an overcast day is more like the neutral light we receive.

It is best to use the cloudy setting when you shoot on cloudy days. This adds warmth and color to your daylight images.

If shooting in the shadows, shade settings are highly recommended. Shaded areas will appear cooler and/or bluer overall, and may require some warmth.

Tungsten settings are best used indoors. This makes it cool and neutralizes yellow tones.

Fluorescent settings help to counter the yellow and green colors often derived form fluorescent light strips.

Flash settings can be used to give your images a cool look and add warmth.

Tips: Make sure to set your white balance manually in order not to have it automatically adjust. This is because the sky can be used to show you what the day looks and help you choose the right color balance. For indoor shots, you will need to consider the lighting conditions and choose the right white balance. Once you take your camera out of its bag, this will become second-nature.

Step 8 Learn how the Histogram is read

The LCD screen is not an accurate way to judge exposure. This is because the image may appear darker than it actually appears on the screen. The histogram, which is a graph located next to your image on your screen, is the best way to verify that the exposure is correct.

Learn how to interpret the thetogram and you'll be able identify the image's range of tones. While this may seem difficult, it's possible to quickly master the histogram. You can use it to take professional photos after a little practice. It is important to remember that the graph shows the shadows, while the graph on the right shows the highlights.

It is important that you note that if your graph is tilted towards the right, the image may be too bright. This can mean that you may lose details in the area of the image's lighter side. Conversely, if you have the image skewed to one side, chances are the image will be underexposed. The photo that results will be too dark.

Step 9 Play around with perspective

The best way to make your photography more interesting is to experiment with different perspectives. You don't have to be on the exact same scene. But if your eyes are open to different angles you can make the most of the situation. You have the option to approach your subject from the top or the bottom, and this can drastically change the look of the photograph.

Realize that not every angle works the same for every photo. It is a fact that you won't find what works if there aren't enough experiments. One example is if you want to photograph wildlife, you could consider going down to their level in order for you to see the world as they see it. To shoot a portrait, however, you might prefer to stand on a platform to view your shot from above.

Step 10 Understanding the Rule of Thirds

The rule of three states that a photo cannot be centered and is therefore considered more interesting and balanced. Now imagine the image that is being captured. The image is covered with a grid. There are two vertical and horizontal lines that divide it into 8 equal parts. This means that you can instead of placing the subject at the centre of your image according to the rule of thirds, but place them at one intersection between the four lines. Some DSLRs allow you to turn grid options on your camera and use them in the composition of your image.

Photography is about creativity. You can break this rule whenever you want to so that the points you are interested in may be at different points. You can do this, but you must be clear about the rules and consider where your desired points should be.

Step 11

When photographing portraits, you will focus your attention on a particular area. This means that sharper images should be your primary concern. The eyes are the most significant facial feature. They are the first thing people notice. This is especially true if people are looking at each other closely.

Keep in mind, your primary focus should be on the eyes of your subject. In order to capture sharp images of your subject's eyes, you need to select one focus point, and aim it towards one of their eyes. Once you have a focus point that is right for one of the eyes you can keep the shutter key half-pressed. Move your DSLR camera closer and you will be able to recompose the image to include the other eye.

Step 12 Pay more attention and pay closer attention to your background

It is important that your background be as simple and uncluttered as possible. It should be clear of clutter wherever possible. It is important that the subject does not draw attention away from it. It is important to choose muted colors or plain patterns for your shoot. Your primary objective is to draw attention to your model, and not to the colorful buildings behind it.

This means you will have to fix distracting background. You can conceal the background by simply using a larger aperture and moving closer to your subject. It is important to keep your background neutral, especially if placing the subject on the right side of your photo.

Step 13 Use a tripod when you can

A tripod is a must-have accessory for getting sharper images in low light. A tripod is ideal for long exposures. This means you can open the shutter for seconds to minutes. This creates incredible effects in your image, such landscapes or waterfalls.

You must therefore consider several factors when buying a tripod. These factors are its height, weight and stability. Weighing the tripod is an important consideration. Because no one likes to carry heavy items around, it's not worth it. But the tripod must also be strong enough for your camera and any lenses you intend to use. Check out the product reviews of other users to get an idea of what they think.

Step 14: Take photos at the sunrise/sunset

Lighting is an important aspect of photography. Understanding the importance of lighting in photography is essential. For photographers, the best times of day are early mornings and late nights. The hour immediately before sunset and the hour after sunrise are known as "the golden hour". This is due to the lower sun's altitude making the light softer and more pleasant.

Shooting portraits or landscapes can create a tranquil feel in your photos, regardless of whether they are taken in the morning or at night. However, this can make your photography easier.

Step 15

Once you know how to shoot RAW images, post-processing will become a necessity. It is crucial that you purchase good photo-editing software. One that allows you to adjust exposure, contrast, white balance, cropping, and getting rid off blemishes.

Lightroom and Adobe Photoshop are two of the most commonly used photo-editing tools by professionals. If your budget is tight, Photoshop Elements and Paint Shop Pro are options.

Step 16

No matter how experienced or talented a photographer may be, everyone takes bad photos. Their portfolios are stunning because they only share the best images. They don't share photos of bad scenes they took when trying to get the best shot.

To make your pieces stand out on social media platforms like Facebook,

Instagram and Twitter, it is essential to choose a few outstanding shots. While you could have taken hundreds or even thousands of photos of the exact same scene, it doesn't mean you should display them all. This might distract from the amazing shots you took.

Step 17: Learn lessons from your mistakes

Photography can be difficult when images are not properly composed, overexposed, or blurry. It is better to not let this frustrate you than to use it as an opportunity for learning. It is impossible to be a good photographer from birth, no matter what your field of expertise. If you are taking bad photos next time, don't rush to delete them. Instead, take time to examine the images and determine the reasons for the problems so that you can figure out the best way of fixing it.

There will always be an easy solution waiting in most cases. There may be a simple solution that involves a new composition or faster shutter speeds. If the problem continues to recur, you may be able to explore other aspects and techniques of photography to help strengthen those areas.

Chapter 9: Factors To Consider When Choosing The Best Dslr Camera

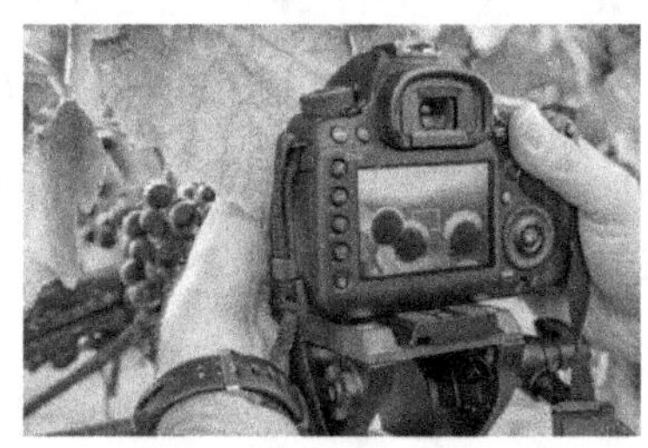

There are many aspects to consider when choosing the right DSLR for your photography. Here are some examples:

Brand

There are many brands that are on the market today, including Canon, Nikon, and The Small Guy. Many people get caught up in these brands and do not know which one is best. Most people are not sure whether to buy a camera from either a big or smaller brand. That shouldn't be your priority. What is most important is that the camera has the features you need.

It is quite true that switching to another brand becomes expensive once you acquire lenses and other accessories. But, it doesn't mean that one brand or another is superior. It is true that Nikon produces great DSLRs but Pentax cameras, Canon and Sony cameras also do. You may think that one brand is superior than another with each new release. But, you will see that the ranks will change next year.

Yes, brands matter. But in most cases they are not the way we like to think. It is more important that you choose a camera for its features than the brand. You must first look into the different accessories and lenses that are available on the market before you can make any purchasing decisions.

To be able to take nature photos, the camera you buy must also have a compatible telescope lens. Canon and Nikon would be the best options. This is due to the fact that they are more familiar and have many flashes, accessories and lenses to choose from. Does this mean you should ignore smaller brands or not buy from them? You should not. Pentax has amazing features, such as weather sealing. These features are hard to find in similar brands at comparable prices.

Sensor Size & Design

The light from a DSLR camera's lens passes through it and hits the sensors. This records the image. These sensors can come in many sizes. You can compare it to the one on your smartphone. However, the sensors in a DSLR camera are much bigger. Because of so many factors, these larger sensors are superior than smaller ones.

The high resolution of the first image you take with a large sensor means that it has a high resolution. This is due to the large size of the sensors, which means that the images are larger and the quality is better. In low light environments, larger sensors will perform better than any other. The amount of light that enters the camera does not change. It simply means that it can collect more light than the camera has the ability to. A larger sensor has the advantage of displaying soft backgrounds and out-offocus backgrounds.

In reality, there are only two sizes of DSLR sensors. The APS-C model is the smaller one, which makes them more accessible to entry-level photographers. This type sensor is commonly found on cameras that can be operated quickly and are affordable.

The full range sensor is the one that measures 35mm in width and larger. The high resolution makes them popular with professional photographers. These could be your best option if you have more than $1600 to spend. But if you're just starting out, this could be a bit too much.

It is possible to ask yourself, "If it seems excessive, why would I mention it?" Many camera sensors are sold either as APS-C or full-frame sensors. If you're looking to grow your skills, you need to consider updating your lenses.

It is vital that you consider the camera's design when choosing the right camera. Backlight sensors are usually designed so that the majority of its buttons can be found at the back. This makes them easy to see. The backlit sensors work better in low-light conditions than the ones that are not.

Today, many camera manufacturers are getting rid optical low pass filters. Others go as far as eliminating anti-aliasing and other filters. This filter has the primary purpose of preventing distortion in patterns. A common example of this filter is a shirt that appears bent and whirled in a photograph.

Sensory technology allows for some degree of distortion to be eliminated without the use of a filter. It is essential to understand that the filter has a main purpose.

Cameras with no optical low pass filter are often more detailed and have richer colours than others. Today's manufacturers are abandoning optical filters completely, as is the case with the Nikon's DSLR. This is because of the important role that enhanced detail plays in fashion or product photos, especially when it comes to clothing boutiques. This is exactly why extra moire is important.

Megapixels

Many people wonder whether the number of pixels is worth taking into consideration when looking to purchase a DSLR. A lot of people buy cameras based only on their megapixels. This is a bad way to decide which camera to get. How much resolution your camera can achieve is determined by the number of megapixels. The megapixels count is determined by multiplying the number of pixels with that on either side. A camera with a larger number of pixels will provide a higher resolution picture than one with a smaller number. This means you can print larger photos without having to crop the image.

However, you need to realize that the megapixels do not matter as much as the sensor's size, especially for image quality. A phone with over 40 MP is not going to be better than a DSLR that only has 16 MP. However, a high resolution phone does not guarantee better images. Apart from the many benefits mentioned, high-megapixel DSLRs increase noise when the ISO value is high. Modern cameras are equipped with high megapixels that can reduce noise.

In addition, larger image files are generated when the megapixel count exceeds 100. This does not have to be a problem because the bigger files generated are more flexible during post-processing. Remember that you will need an extra large external drive and a bigger SD card to store the high-megapixel photos.

Speed shooting

A camera's shooting speed is the speed at which you can take a photograph. In sports photography, and for actions, it is vital to make sure your camera has a high speed shooting speed. You should prioritize speed if your goal is continuous photography. This is mainly due to the fact speed is crucial when it concerns capturing action and the best expressions.

It is sometimes difficult to measure the speed and acceleration of a camera with a pencil. Camera speed can be gauged by its burst speed as well as the number photos per second it can take. If you decide to keep the shutter closed, this is an indication of the camera's overall speed.

Moving parts of a DSLR camera is necessary for every photo. This mirror mechanism is what many camera's lack. Consider large images as it can take some time for digital photos to be processed by a camera, especially if they have a higher resolution. The burst speed on many DSLRs is about five frames per second. That means it can take around five photos per minute.

The higher number of photos a camera takes in a second, means that you are more likely to capture a perfect moment. However, the camera's burst speeds may be indicative of how fast it generally operates.

The type of photography that you want to do will determine the speed you need. A DSLR running at 10 fps in burst mode is great for sports, wildlife, and action photos. This is because you can capture more perfect moments with a slower burst speed.

You also need to pay attention at shutter speed. The shutter speed will determine how long the shutter is open to capture a shot. If you have an affordable DSLR, a 1/4000 shutter speeds is sufficient to freeze actions. It also works well for many types of photography. Advanced models have a shutter speed of 1/16,000. You should remember that the faster your shutter speed is, the more light you need. They can be useful for shooting outdoors on very sunny days, with a wide aperture to ensure that the image does not get too dark.

Price of a DSLR Camera for Beginners

Many people are unaware that they're not buying the most expensive camera on the market. They're simply getting the one that fits their style and is within their budget. There are many DSLRs out there, and the cost of them is very similar to small cars. You get many advanced features with them. But, you can find them for only a few hundreds dollars. They do a decent job. They can be used for beginner photographers and are very simple to learn.

The entry-level/beginner DSLRs cost as low as $300. Some of them are very realistic. The range of prices is $500-

1000. As you add new features such as shutter speed, pixels, and more, your price will go up.

You don't need a brand new DSLR if you don't have enough cash. However, you can buy an older model that still has the features that you desire. It is important that you understand that older DSLR models are still excellent cameras. Most of the time, it is possible to get a cheaper mid-level DSLR. The entry-level features are also easy to use for beginners.

It is vital that you look at the features in addition to the price. This is because a new camera will likely offer an improvement in image quality. A model older than a year does not make a difference to the new one. If the model is more than two years old, the quality of the image will be less if it is not properly set.

Kit Lens and Camera Body

After you have decided on the DSLR camera that you want to purchase, the next step is to choose whether or not to buy the camera body. A DSLR camera with a set lens has been the preferred choice of many beginners. Kit lenses are great as they cover most zoom ranges between 18mm and 56mm. They are inexpensive and ideal for beginners interested learning about photography.

However, it's important to remember that the lens included in a kit lens is usually very small. This is due to their maximum aperture being f/3.6. You might be curious about what the aperture does in photography. The truth is that aperture has a significant impact on how large the lens opening is. Because of this, a wider aperture will result in better results when shooting in low light conditions. It also allows for softer out-of focus backgrounds. This can make a significant difference in the quality of your images. The cost can increase significantly, too.

Chapter 10: Understanding The Elements Of Exposure

Let's talk about the basics of exposure. It is important to remember three things when it comes down to exposure: ISO, shutter speed and aperture. Let's have a closer look at those three items.

There is a hole in the lens of every camera that lets light through. The aperture is the name of this opening.

A shutter inside the camera acts as a keypad. The shutter can be opened to allow light to pass through during the photo taking process. The shutter closes and light cannot enter the aperture. The shutter can be set by your DSLR camera to open or close for as long as you like. Shutter-speed measures how long the shutter is open.

Digital cameras include a sensor that controls the camera's sensitivity to sunlight. The ISO setting (light sensitivity control) is what you call it.

Let's have a closer look at these three parts.

Aperture

Aperture, or a hole inside a lens, allows light to enter the camera. The size and direction of the opening will affect how much light the camera can receive at any given point. A small opening can let very little light through the camera, while large openings allow lots of light to get in.

By changing the F Stops in a camera, you can control the aperture size. F-Stops may be viewed on the viewfinder or control screen. It should be possible to identify the setting by the number F, preceded only by the letter F.

In order to adjust the aperture settings, your camera must be set up in manual mode. Most DSLR cameras come with a dial on the top of their camera bodies that can be turned on manual mode. The letter M is used to denote this setting. To change the aperture value shown on the screen or in viewfinder, simply rotate this dial.

What is F-Stop? F-Stop, which is the focal length divided with the aperture opening of a lens, basically means that the lens's focal length is divided by its aperture. This is a confusing term for most photographers. The aperture opening will be smaller if the F number is higher. A smaller aperture opening equals a lower F number. This is a chart that shows F-Stops.

Some cameras have the ability to adjust between full stops. This allows for finer tuning. You should remember that every stop permits twice as much light than the previous stop.

It is important to know that different lenses have different apertures. The optional lenses you mount to your DSLR will change the camera's aperture availability. The focal length determines how the aperture can be adjusted.

Depth Of Field (DOF), which is a term denoting the distance between closest and furthest objects, in an image. Depth of Field will be affected by how you adjust your aperture. Here's how this works:

The greater the F number, the smaller is the opening (f/22) = higher DOF

The smaller F Number means a larger opening (f/2) = Less DOF

Practically speaking, a photo taken at a higher aperture setting like f/22 has more background in focus. A photograph taken with an aperture setting of f/2 or lower will have blurry backgrounds.

Shutter Speed

Shutter speed is simply the time that the shutter is opened. You can't live without knowing how to use shutter speeds to your advantage, no matter how long the shutter is open.

As we saw with aperture, a shutter is like an open door. It is comprised of two parts, which we will call curtain C and curtain A. When the shutter button is pressed, curtain A rises in order to let light enter the camera. Curtain B then rises up to meet curtain B and both of them reset to their original positions.

DSLR cameras come with an additional step. There is an additional step in DSLR cameras. A mirror that is at 45 degrees to the shutter reflects light onto the viewfinder. When you fire the shutter release, the mirror rises, allowing light in to the shutter. After that, the shutter returns to its original function.

It may seem complicated but this is the basic understanding of how shutter speed works. But how do you use shutter speed in order to take amazing pictures? Here are three methods that shutter speed can be used to your advantage:

1. Shutters let light in from your scene into the camera. Because shutters are open, you can see the effects on the image.

2. A fast shutter speed can freeze fast action objects like cars racing or athletes competing.

3. Slow shutter speeds enable you to adjust the lighting while keeping your shutter open. This will allow you to create amazing effects in your photos. It is easier to capture the movement behind your subject if you use a slower shutter speed.

One example is if you were taking a photo of a dancer mid-move. A fast shutter speed would just freeze the moment and lose all of the essence of what is happening. A slower shutter speed would enable you to capture movement as there would still be some blur. Moving vehicles can achieve the same effect.

The shutter speed is typically located close to the shutter release button on your camera's top, but it can vary depending on brand.

Important tip about shutter speed. You might notice that your pictures don't look as sharp if you are holding the camera with one hand and not using a tripod. Cameras can blur an image if the shutter speed is too slow. This happens even if you have a pulse. This will prevent you from having to change your shutter speed. For example, if your lens is 50mm, you would use 1/100thof a second. It may not always be the case, as some people are extremely steady, while others are less steady. Keep making small adjustments until the problem is solved.

ISO

ISO is an important tool that can help with your photography. It is often overlooked and misunderstood. It was back when film rolls were invented that they could be labeled using a film speed like 100, 200, 400, and so on. The higher numbers were called "faster" film while lower numbers were called "slower" film. People mistakenly assumed that fast film was intended for photographing fast moving objects such a race car or a baseball pitch. Slow film was intended for stills as well as slow moving objects.

The film speed was actually the speed at the which the film responded to light. Film speed refers to how quickly it reacts when exposed to light. It had nothing in common with the speed the subject was moving.

You can capture amazing photos even when the light isn't very bright with higher ISO settings. However, using high ISO settings can cause noise and graininess in some images. This is the most obvious problem with low quality DSLR cameras.

Notice how the picture on its right has a brighter, higher ISO setting. The image to the left looks darker and more yellow.

Your camera's ISO setting may be a better option than flashing in low light conditions. Flashes tend to add harshness to the subject which can be unflattering. It is possible to make low-light photos sharper, more balanced by simply turning off the flash.

Understanding Depth in Field

What are you most likely to focus on in a picture? The human brain is trained to focus on the best part of an image. Photographers should remember that when they are taking pictures, they must be focused on the point they want attention to.

If you're taking a portrait of someone else, make sure that the subject is the focus point. This includes their face. This concept is applicable when the background is too busy to focus on your subject. Blurring the background can help draw the attention to the subject. This technique can also be useful if you want to highlight one subject from a group.

Depth of field (DOF), also known as the distance between distant and nearest objects in a scene, is a measure of how sharp an image appears. There are three main factors that affect depth of field.

Aperture opening is the most important. The larger the aperture opening (remember that it is the smaller F numbers! The lower your field depth, the greater it will be. The wider your aperture is, the deeper the field.

The focal length of a lens is also an important factor in depth of fields. Lenses with longer focal lengths will produce less depth of the field, while lenses of shorter focal lengths provide greater depth.

The third factor that affects depth-of-field is the distance between the subject and the camera. A closer distance to the subject means less depth of coverage. You will get more depth of the field if your subject is closer.

Camera Modes

The five modes available in most entry-level DSLR camera models are Manual, Aperture priority, Shutter priority, Program, and Auto. These modes may be identified by different letters and symbols. Refer to the manual of your camera for details about how these modes are labeled.

Auto Mode

The first mode we'll look at is Auto mode. The factory presets are used to control the camera's settings in Auto mode. The camera controls shutter speed as well as ISO, aperture, flash, and all other settings. Auto mode is not as controllable as you might think. Unfortunately, amateur photographers who use this mode too often are disappointed with their images.

Program Mode

You can change the program mode to gain more control over camera functions. Program Mode still allows the camera to set the shutter speed or aperture. However, it can be used to adjust things such as ISO, whitebalance, exposure compensation and use of flash. This mode is less versatile than Auto Mode but can still give you excellent results.

Priority Shutter

Shutter Priority Mode allows for you to adjust your shutter speed while the aperture is set by the camera. You'll need to watch the F number in your camera's display to ensure sufficient light is available for the shutter speed that you choose. Most cameras display "Lo" when there is not enough lighting for the shutter speed set. This will lead to extremely dark photos. The camera sensor will detect too much light and produce dark photos. Depending upon the brand, the aperture will display "Hi" and similar messages.

Shutter Priority mode may be used when shutter speeds are the most important component of your photo. For example, when you take pictures of fast moving subjects, the shutter speed must be fast enough for blur to not occur. A slower shutter speed will produce blurry images.

Priority: Aperture

Aperture priority is the next option. This is the reverse mode of Shutter Priority. Instead of using shutter speed, the camera will automatically assign shutter speed to you. The shutter speed that is assigned by the camera in this mode should be something you pay attention too. If you're holding the camera by your hand, make sure that the shutter speed does not go too slow. It can cause camera-shake distortions.

If aperture is the main element of the photo, then Aperture Priority mode can be used. This is where you'll find your preferred depth of focus. What do you want? A blurred background or focus on your subject? These choices are what determine aperture settings.

Manual Mode

Manual mode is the final mode we'll examine. Manual mode allows you full control of all aspects of the camera's operation. This mode can help you achieve the exact composition you want for your shots. For very unique photos, experiment with various aperture settings and shutter speeds.

Do not be afraid to test out the various modes to see how they affect your photos. The modes allow you to quickly become familiar with all aspects of the camera's operations without feeling overwhelmed.

Characteristics and characteristics of light

This chapter discusses light, which is one the most important aspects of photography. Photographers must have the ability to see and utilize light in order for them to be able take the best pictures.

You might think that you cannot judge the right lighting for your shot. But you can train your eye to see light properly and use it to your advantage in your photographs. The key is to learn what you're looking for in light.

Direction of Light

It is important to understand from where the light is coming. Light can shine from the sides, back, or front of your subject. The direction that the light comes from can dramatically affect the shot. You can use this information to change the mood.

Front lighting is the most used type. This type lighting is often preferred by amateur photographers as it highlights the subject and makes it easy to use. It is also popular due to the fact that many novice photographers are not confident enough in their abilities to try other lighting techniques.

Front lighting uses light from behind the photographer to shine directly onto the subject. This position illuminates most of the scene. It is possible to eliminate shadows by using front lighting, although this is not always the best option. Shadows can give photos a 3-D look and keep them from looking flat.

Minimal shadows, on the other hand can be helpful in reducing texture and detail. This may make portrait subjects more attractive.

A side effect of front lighting is that your subject may squint. This can make capturing natural shots difficult.

Back lighting is another option when lighting your subjects. As you would imagine, the subject gets lit from the back while the light source points towards the camera. It is great for creating silhouettes. You can create very mysterious and interesting photos by using the rim-light effect.

Side lighting is a third option to lighting your subject. Side lighting gives photos dimension and deep shadows. But, you should be aware that deep shadows are not always flattering for your subject.

For the best shots, it is important to control the lighting. Consider the different features and shapes of your subject before you place your light source.

It can be simpler to use a flash or other strobe light to direct the light in the desired direction. If you are using natural lighting, such as sunlight or moonlight, you need to rotate the subject to achieve the lighting effect that you want.

Diffusion of Light

Lighting can also be diffused to different degrees. There are two options for lighting.

If there is strong light, the contrast between the darks (and lights) of a photograph will be high. The shadows can be very dark and the brighter areas very bright. This can add a 3D effect to a picture.

Contrast between the dark and light areas of a photograph in soft light is much lower than that found in brighter lighting. The subject tends glowier, with a soft transition of shadows and lit areas.

Hard light situations include indoor photography, outdoors when there is more sunlight and indoor photography that is closer to the subject. The golden hours are approximately an hour after sunrise or an hour before sunset. This time of the day has an amazing quality of light, it is bright and colorful, with a lovely golden glow.

For dramatic portraits, hard side lighting is a favourite of photographers. As the light wraps around the subject, the brighter side will become shadows.

The following are examples of situations that favor soft lighting:

Outdoor photos of subjects taken on cloudy day, subjects in shaded areas, and indoor scenes lit by window lights. Window lighting is an excellent choice for baby portraits.

The color temperature of light

One type of light may be brighter than another. It is a term that means the light has more yellow or warmer tones. Cooler light refers light that is more blue.

Different light sources produce different color temperatures. Shade tends toward bluer and/or cooler tones. Direct sunlight will generally produce warmer tones.

The time of day affects how the light colors look. Photos taken during golden hour will have a warm hue. Cooler tones can be seen in pictures taken at dusk after the sun has set. You can have starkly different colors for the same subject depending upon the temperature of your lighting.

Artificial light sources also can produce different color temperatures. Fluorescent lighting will produce a cooler hue than tungsten, which can be yellower and more warm.

Understanding the white balance
White balance is simply a way to control the color temperature within your photos. It can be tempting for novice photographers to leave their camera on automatic white balance and allow the camera itself to adjust. This might work fine in outdoor conditions, but indoors, it is a problem.
Human eyes can adapt to different lighting conditions, and still see the object's true color. A camera cannot see the true color of an object in every lighting situation. A camera will most likely see a yellowish-colored sheet of paper, such as a white sheet made

from copy paper. For more accuracy, it may need to balance the color.

A DSLR camera can use a variety of presets to adjust white balance, including: Incandescent or Fluorescent, Direct sunlight, Flash, Shadow, Cloudy, or Flash. It is important to match the white light mode with your current setting.

If you are in an area lit by incandescent light, you can set the camera's white to Incandescent. This will adjust the camera's white balance to compensate for the yellowish-colored incandescent lighting. The majority of indoor sporting events are under bright fluorescent lighting, which can produce a greenish hue in the photos. You can fix this problem by changing the white mode to Fluorescent.

In most cases, an auto white balance will work fine in outdoor settings. You will need to customize the white equilibrium for all other situations. The gray card, also known as a gray card, is required to customize white balance. A gray card is simply a small square card in gray that the camera will perceive as neutral. It is possible to create a custom White Balance depending on your camera brand. To learn more about how to do this, you can consult the manual of your camera.

This is how it works: you use the card to tell the camera it's a neutral colour and then it will adjust all other colors to match. Put the gray card in a similar light that you use to photograph your subject. Take a photo of the card to show how the camera adjusts the other colors.

If you don't own a gray card, you can use a piece of paper instead. This is not the ideal solution, but it can work. Most cameras can save up to five presets, which can come in handy if you plan on taking pictures at multiple locations.

Metering modes
What is metering, exactly? Metering can be described as the process by which your DSLR camera determines the amount of light within a frame. Then, it adjusts the ISO, shutter speed or aperture parameters to achieve the desired exposure.
The reason that metering is necessary is because DSLR cameras have a very primitive view compared to the human eyes. You could think of yourself as a photographer. Your subject's face will be shadowed and darkened by the bright background due to your light position. Human eyes are more capable of automatically adjusting the brightness and increasing the exposure of the subject to achieve a clear view. A camera, by contrast, can only "see" one exposure

in a shot. To control the exposure, you have to tell it which elements to adjust. Is it supposed to adjust to the subject, the background lighting or the main source of light? Metering control is what makes it so important.

Default Metering

The default setting is the best option for metering modes. This is the setting most people start using when they first get started with photography. It's also known by the evaluative and multi-zone meters. The camera will use this mode to break up the scene into different zones. Each zone will be able to provide information regarding the brightness or darkness. It will also consider any active autofocus points and give a bias to the light levels within those areas. This combination allows the camera to calculate the exposure needed for the desired shot. The default setting works best with shots that are generally well lit without any extremes.

Center Weighted Metering

The next option is center weighted measuring. This metering mode evaluates the entire frame. However it biases toward the center of a frame by about 60 to 80 per cent. This mode can be used when the background of the subject has large areas that are darkened. It will cause the camera's exposure to be increased in the central area, making them too bright.

Spot Metering

Spot meters are the next most common metering mode, after evaluative metering or default. They can give you the exact look that your shots need. The camera uses this mode to measure the amount of light in the area around the auto focus point. It then uses that information to calculate the exposure settings of the focal point. The best thing about this mode, however, is the ability to adjust your aperture settings to take full control of the lighting in your photo.

In summary, DSLR metering mode are very primitive in comparison to the human eye's ability to compensate different exposures within a scene. These options allow you to have complete control over your camera and tell the camera what you want it to do with a particular shot. You'll be able capture better shots in the beginning and save time editing afterwards.

Photo Composition

Composition is the most important aspect. It doesn't matter how technical you are with exposure, white balance, lighting and so on. But if your composition looks bad and boring, it will look professional. There are many ways to improve your photo composition.

Rule of thirds

The most well-known composition rule is the Rule to Thirds. It can also be called the Golden Ratio. It is as simple as imagining your photo divided into three equal horizontal and vertical parts. It is important to place the key elements of your photograph wherever the imaginary lines cross in the photo.

The Rule of Thirds helps you create beautiful pictures that are balanced and easy on the eyes. It is also extremely helpful when taking portraits. Portraits of people are often about the subject's eyes. The subject's eyes should be placed at the intersections of imaginary lines. This will draw the viewers' attention to that point in an interesting manner.

Symmetry

Symmetry is a technique that can be used in place of the Rule of Thirds. This rule puts the subject in the middle. From the subject's edge to the center of the photo, there should be an equal distance. This rule focuses on drawing your eye to the subject.

Balancing Elements
Sometimes, using the Rule of Thirds may make certain parts of the photograph feel a bit empty. In this instance, you would add additional elements to your background to balance the picture. This can be used to give the photo a 3D feel.
Background Simplicity
There will be times when your background needs to be kept as simple as possible. This is especially true if you do not want the background to distract the viewer. These types of photos work well with a black or pure-white background.
Lines
It is possible to make important decisions about the composition of a

picture by using different lines. There are many situations where lines can be drawn. You can use lines to guide the viewer towards the subject, or even draw them in. There are many options for lines to use in your photo. Curved line can also be very appealing, as in a path that leads to a house or a beach cottage.

Patterns

It is a good idea also to pay attention any patterns you may be noticing. Many patterns can make for beautiful and complex compositions. It can also make interesting backgrounds for your subject.

Depth

Despite the fact our world is three-dimensional and photos are two-dimensional it's possible to still create the illusion depth in your photographs through your composition. A picture can have a lot more depth if it has a foreground as well as a middle ground and background.

Framing

You can find many fascinating and interesting frames in the world. Natural frames are a great method to draw attention to the main theme of the photograph. Natural frames can include foliage, holes in a wall, and anything else. The possibilities are limitless and allow for amazing photography.

Depth in the Field

If we use a shallow depth, it can draw the attention of the viewer to our subject. We naturally draw our eyes to the focal point in the scene. Also, a shallow depth can help to eliminate distracters that might be lurking in the background.

Reflections

Also, reflections can add an interesting element to any composition. It's actually one the most common compositional elements among experienced photographers. Reflections can be found all over the place. Reflections can be found everywhere, including in water, mirrors and shiny objects. Shadows are another type, and they can play an important part in compositions. They add mystery or excitement to photos.

Horizon Positioning

Photograph compositions are incomplete without the importance of the horizon. Amateur photographers most often make the common mistake of placing horizons in the middle. It is possible to do this in very specific situations. However, generally speaking it is a bad idea. This is because it confuses a viewer's eyes. It doesn't know which way to go.

Before taking a photo, determine which part of the composition you think is most important. If you want to capture a dramatic skyline, place the horizon in third. If the ground element of your photograph is the most important then you can place the horizontal line in the top-third. Unless you are trying to achieve an odd effect, it is essential that the horizontal line is straight.

Good composition is key to highlighting your subject. It's something every photographer should strive to achieve. Good composition is also very pleasing to your eyes. You should know exactly what you want from the photo before you begin shooting. This will allow for you to create pleasing compositions.

Focus: Auto and manual

Many times, new photographers experience difficulties with focusing. If the subject is not in center of the shot, it can make it difficult to focus. Perhaps you were confused by all the available focus modes. This section will help answer these questions and many other issues related to focusing your DSLR.

There are two types main types of focus: autofocus and manual focus. Understanding how to switch between these two modes is the first thing you should do. You will need to refer to your owner's manual to determine the exact location. However you should generally find a switch on your camera with the labels M for manual focus and AF for automatic focus. Turn the switch to the desired mode to get started.

Optional lenses may also have their own focus switch. You will notice a slight variation in the way that it is labeled. The label M/A and the M on a lens are usually used to tell it to use the same settings as its focus setting. M can be used to manually focus a lens without the use of the camera.

Auto Focus Points

Sharpness is one of the key standards in digital photography. Sharpness is a key component of a good photograph. Although it may seem counter intuitive, beginners can find the autofocus feature of the camera confusing. It causes them almost to stick to the center point. It is possible to miss out on other autofocus points which can create beautiful pictures.

Auto focus points refer to the small boxes you see in the viewfinder of your camera when you press the shutter halfway.

The camera automatically chooses which box of autofocus point to use when it is in auto mode. If you are in another mode, like aperture priority or another programme mode, you can pick your own focus point.

Why should you not use the centre auto focus point? It's the fastest and most accurate focal point, right? While the center focal point is generally the most accurate and fastest, the quality or the camera can affect the accuracy of any other autofocus points. Because we want to place the main subject in a different location than the centre of the shot, we do not always use the center focus point. We try to get more interest from our photographs than that.

In order to get a better shot, amateur photographers may do the following: First, place the center autofocus box on the main subject. Then, press the shutter key halfway down to signal that the subject is in focus. You can then move your camera to get the composition you want while keeping the subject focused.

This technique has the disadvantage of changing the light entering the shot and the camera inadvertently. Using the focus and composition method can often lead to adverse effects on the shot.

You can use one of your camera's alternate autofocus points to compose your shot. This will allow you to focus the camera on the main subject, without worrying about changing the exposure. Although it can take some practice getting used to the idea of changing your focus points, it becomes a natural part of your camera's routine.

Manual Focus

Manual focus is a different option to auto focus. Instead of having the camera do the focusing automatically, the photographer can take complete control.

What situations is it more beneficial to use manual focus over auto focus? Most commonly, manual focal is used in the following situations.

1. Macro or Closeup photography - Very important for capturing details in this kind of photography.

2. Low Light Environments - Low light can have a negative impact on the auto focus of your camera.

3. Obstruction in Scene- The camera can't auto focus on the intended subject if there is a barrier, such a glass door or fence between it and the subject.

4. Action Photography: Shooting fast moving subjects using autofocus modes can be frustrating.

5. Panorama shots - Manual focus is better than autofocus when you are taking panorama photos. Because you want to preserve the same depth of field in every individual shot, you need to make sure the panorama has the same depth.

6. Reflection Images: A reflection, especially with shiny subject matter, can cause your camera not to focus in auto mode.

7. Lack of Contrast. If the shot does not contain any major contrasting

colors, it will be very difficult for the camera to auto focus the image. The camera is unable pick out particular points within a composition.

Manual focus is preferred by many photographers. This is because manual focus allows for complete control of one of the most important aspects of a photograph. Picture sharpness may be the most desired characteristic in any photograph.

Once you are proficient in manual focus, you'll notice an increase in artistic quality and a greater satisfaction with your pictures. Try both manual and auto focus. They are both excellent at different aspects.